NEW
EVANGELISATION

**Other books by Archbishop Porteous
published by Connor Court/Modotti Press**

After the Heart of God: the Life and Ministry of Priests at the Beginning of the Third Millennium (2009)

A New Wine & Fresh Skins: Ecclesial Movements in the Church (2010)

Streams of Grace, Spiritual Movements That Shaped the Church (2011)

Become What You Are, Growing in Christian Character (2012)

New Evangelisation

Pastoral Strategy for the Church
at the beginning of the Third Millennium

Julian Porteous

Connor Court Publishing
Ballatat

Published in 2014 by Connor Court Publishing Pty Ltd
Copyright © Julian Porteous 2014

ALL RIGHTS RESERVED. This book contains material protected under International and Federal Copyright Laws and Treaties. Any unauthorised reprint or use of this material is prohibited. No part of this book may be reproduced or transmitted in any form or by any means, electronic or mechanical, including photocopying, recording, or by any information storage and retrieval system without express written permission from the publisher.

PO Box 224W
Ballarat VIC 3350
sales@connorcourt.com
www.connorcourt.com

ISBN: 9781925138252 (pbk.)

Cover design by M. Giordano

Printed in Australia

Dedicated to St John Paul II

CONTENTS

Preface

1. First Christian Proclamation of the Gospel — 1
2. The Message: Preaching the Crucified Christ — 17
3. A Brief History of Evangelisation — 29
4. The New Cultural Landscape — 46
5. Church Teaching on Evangelisation — 70
6. A New Evangelisation — 88
7. Keys to the New Evangelisation — 101
8. Preaching the New Evangelisation — 116
9. Fostering the Christian Life — 142
10. Role of the Lay Person in the New Evangelisation — 152
11. Methods of Evangelisation — 164
12. Transforming the Culture — 194
13. A New Springtime — 218

Afterword — 222

Preface

As a young newly ordained priest, Pope Paul VI's Apostolic Exhortation, *Evangelii Nuntiandi*,[1] had a profound effect on me. As I read it I saw the nature of the mission of the Church presented in a clear and decisive manner. In essence, the mission of the Church was to proclaim Jesus Christ to the world and to enable people to enter into a real and personal relationship with him. It gave clarity and direction to my priestly ministry. Prior to ordination I'd had some spiritual experiences which drew me into a personal relationship with God. For these experiences I have always been grateful as they were completely unmerited graces by which God revealed his personal love for me. They lit a fire in my heart that has never gone out.

This book brings together my developing understanding of what evangelisation entails. I have been inspired along the way by papal teaching. It gives expression to what I have experienced over a period of some 40 years of being actively involved in various works of evangelisation. It gives expression to my deep conviction that the New Evangelisation must be the pastoral strategy for the Church as it enters the third millennium of Christianity.

Archbishop Julian Porteous,

Archbishop of Hobart

12 January 2014

Feast of the Baptism of the Lord

---

1 *Evangelii Nuntiandi* was written by Pope Paul VI in the light of the Synod of Bishops who met to discuss the subject of evangelisation. The Synod took place in Rome in October 1974 and the Exhortation was promulgated in December 1975.

1

First Christian Proclamation of the Gospel

The first proclamation of the Christian Gospel occurred on the day of Pentecost when St Peter stood up before a crowd which had gathered outside of the upper room. He came out of the room and preached to the assembled people. The evangelising mission of the Church had begun.

There is a significant link between the coming of the Holy Spirit upon the Apostles at Pentecost and the work of evangelisation. To understand this link we need to consider the final instructions of the Lord to his Apostles at the time of his ascension. Jesus, the risen Lord, appeared to his disciples on a number of occasions after his resurrection.[1] These appearances took place over a period of some 40 days. The final time he was to appear to his disciples he asked them to meet him on a hillside named Olivet outside Jerusalem. St Luke records the event twice – once in his Gospel (Luke 24:46-53) and

---

[1] The New Testament recounts that after his resurrection Jesus made a number of appearances to his disciples. After appearing to Mary Magdalene in the Garden (John 20:11-18) the risen Lord appeared in the upper room (John 20:19-29), along the road to Emmaus (Luke 24:13-32) and beside the Sea of Galilee (John 21:1-23). His final appearance is reported as being forty days after the resurrection when he ascended into heaven (Luke 24:44-49). In 1 Corinthians, St Paul records that the risen Lord "appeared to Cephas, then to the twelve" (15:5); "then he appeared to more than five hundred brethren at one time, most of whom are still alive, though some have fallen asleep" (15:6); "then he appeared to James; then of all the Apostles" (15:7). St Paul then adds, "Last of all, as to one untimely born, he appeared also to me" (15:8-9) – a reference to his encounter on the road to Damascus recorded in Acts 9:3-9.

once in the Acts of the Apostles (Acts 1:8-11). The Ascension of the Lord is also recorded in St Mark's Gospel (16:19-20).

Both St Mark and St Matthew record that Jesus gave the instruction to his disciples that they were to go out to "all the world" and "make disciples of all the nations". St Matthew expresses this Great Commission in these words: "Go therefore and make disciples of all nations, baptising them in the name of the Father and of the Son and of the Holy Spirit, teaching them to observe all that I have commanded you" (Matthew 28:19-20). In the Acts of the Apostles Jesus commands his disciples to be his witnesses "in Jerusalem and in all Judea and Samaria and to the end of the earth" (Acts 1:8). St Mark records: "So then the Lord Jesus, after he had spoken to them, was taken up into heaven, and sat down at the right hand of God. And they went forth and preached everywhere, while the Lord worked with them and confirmed the message by the signs that attended it. Amen" (Mark 16:19-20).

The New Testament clearly records that Jesus entrusted the mission of proclaiming the message of salvation "to the ends of the earth". The Ascension of the Lord marks the completion of his earthly mission. As he is about to ascend to his Father he entrusts to his disciples the responsibility of continuing his mission. The mission of Jesus is now the mission of the Church.

However there was another instruction that he gave to his disciples at this time. It is St Luke who tells us of this instruction: "And behold, I send the promise of my Father upon you; but stay in the city, until you are clothed with power from on high" (Luke 24:49). St Luke records that after witnessing the Ascension of the Lord the disciples returned to Jerusalem and gathered in the upper room – the same room where they had celebrated the Last Supper with Jesus – in obedience to his instruction and awaited the fulfilment of this promise.

What was the significance of this second instruction? In one sense it seems to conflict with the Great Commission. We seem to have two opposing instructions – go out/wait. Why did the Lord ask his disciples to wait?

One would have thought that they were ready to carry out the mission entrusted to them: they had been with Jesus for about three years. They had witnessed his miracles, evidence of the power of God at work in him. They had been in the crowds spellbound as they listened to him speak. They had come to realise that Jesus of Nazareth was indeed the Messiah that the Jewish people had been awaiting for many centuries. They had witnessed him risen from the dead. One would have thought that they were ready to carry out this mission. At one level they were – they understood who he was and believed in him. They had received much instruction, both in the crowds who gathered to listen to him and in more personal private moments when he took his disciples aside.

However, Jesus knew that they were not ready just yet. He knew that they lacked the courage and confidence to carry out this mission. At the time of his passion and death the disciples had shown the fragility of their courage. They had run away when Jesus was arrested. Peter, their leader, had betrayed him. The cruel fate of their master hung over them. We are told by St John that they used to lock the door of the room where they met "for fear of the Jews".[2] They were frightened and lacked the zeal to enable them to confront their own people with the truth about Jesus of Nazareth. The Lord knew that unless they were able to overcome this fear they would not be able to carry out his mission. That is why he told them to wait till they were "clothed with power from on high".

---

2 See John 20:19.

On Pentecost Day the promise of Jesus was fulfilled as the Holy Spirit came upon the disciples. They were wonderfully transformed. Immediately after the Holy Spirit came down upon them St Peter went out, opened the doors of the room where they were gathered, and began to preach the first Christian proclamation. St Peter declared: "Let all the house of Israel therefore know assuredly that God has made him both Lord and Christ, this Jesus whom you crucified" (Acts 2:36). The first Christian preaching announced the meaning of the death and resurrection of Jesus Christ. We are told by St Luke that his listeners were "cut to the heart" and 3,000 people were converted and baptised (Acts 2:37).

After describing in some detail the proclamation of St Peter, the final section of this chapter in the Acts of the Apostles provides St Luke's description of the first Christian community in Jerusalem:

> And they devoted themselves to the Apostles' teaching and fellowship, to the breaking of bread and the prayers. And fear came upon every soul; and many wonders and signs were done through the Apostles. And all who believed were together and had all things in common; and they sold their possessions and goods and distributed them to all, as any had need. And day by day, attending the temple together and breaking bread in their homes, they partook of food with glad and generous hearts, praising God and having favour with all the people. And the Lord added to their number day by day those who were being saved (Acts 2:42-47).

In chapter 2 of the Acts of the Apostles we see an important paradigm: the action of the Holy Spirit; the bold preaching of the message; conversion of hearers and the formation of the Christian community (the Church).

There is an intrinsic link between the Holy Spirit and evangelisation and the Church. Without the coming of the Holy Spirit at Pentecost the Church would not have been born. In every age the mission of the Church is able to be carried out because the Holy Spirit is an active presence in the ministry of the Church. The disciples knew in their minds what they needed to tell the world, but they needed a fire in their hearts to enable them to boldly proclaim the message.

The Christian Gospel is a message that is to be conveyed to the mind. It is the truth about God's action in history in the sending of his Son. The Gospel contains an essential intellectual content. However, the effective proclamation of the Gospel needs to be more than just an intellectual understanding of its content and truth. The proclamation of the Gospel requires a certain boldness and zeal. The Gospel is proclaimed by preachers whose hearts are on fire. That fire is enkindled by the Holy Spirit.

The history of the Church records times of evangelical fervour where there is a discernible movement of the Holy Spirit enabling bold and effective Christian proclamation.

The Holy Spirit and evangelisation

The Holy Spirit plays a vital role in evangelisation. The images of the presence and activity of the Spirit described by St Luke can assist us in understanding how the Holy Spirit is linked to evangelisation.

St Luke tells us that as the Spirit came upon the disciples at Pentecost they heard a sound that filled the entire house where they were sitting (Acts 2:1). St Luke describes the sound that "came from heaven like the rush of a mighty wind". This phenomenon provides a source of reflection on the nature of the Holy Spirit in the Christian life. When we consider this image of the Holy Spirit as wind we are reminded about the nature of the wind. We cannot see the wind, but we know the wind is blowing by the effects that the wind has. While the wind is invisible we see it causing trees to move and items to run on the ground.

In a similar way we cannot see the Spirit but we can identify the presence and activity of the Spirit by the effects that the Spirit has in the lives of believers. At Pentecost the Holy Spirit had a transforming effect on the disciples and empowered them with the confidence and courage to evangelise.

We speak of the "gifts of the Spirit". The presence of the Spirit is identified not so much in himself as rather by the gifts he bestows on us. There are a number of lists of the gifts of the Spirit found in Sacred Scripture. These are in no way meant to be complete lists. They are sample lists of the way the Spirit of God can imbue us with spiritual capacities. Catholics would be familiar with the seven gifts of the Spirit associated with the Sacrament of Confirmation: wisdom, understanding, knowledge, right judgement, courage, reverence and fear of the Lord. This list of gifts comes from the writings of the prophet Isaiah who presents these gifts as qualities of the Messiah.[3] This list of gifts proposes that the Holy Spirit will foster those qualities in the Christian which are required to enable to Christian to live like Christ (the Messiah). This list of gifts witnesses to the inner spiritual transformation which the Spirit brings to the Christian.

Several of the gifts – wisdom, knowledge, understanding and right judgement – are gifts associated with the mind. They reflect the promise of Jesus that the Spirit would lead the Christian in the ways of truth. Jesus promised, "When the Spirit of truth comes, he will guide you into all truth" (John 16:13). The Holy Spirit acts in the mind lifting it from earthly wisdom to an ability to grasp divine truth.

---

3 See Isaiah 11:2-3.

Hence a person of faith will be able to perceive things according to the mind of God. This capacity will enable the Christian to proclaim the "things of the Spirit" to people whose thinking is limited by earthly preoccupations. In his Letter to the Romans St Paul comments: "For those who live according to the flesh set their minds on the things of the flesh, but those who live according to the Spirit set their minds on the things of the Spirit" (Romans 8:5).

St Paul provides a list of charismata – special spiritual gifts – in his First Letter to the Corinthians. He mentions the gifts of preaching and teaching, of prophesy and miracles, of faith and discernment, and the gift of tongues (1 Corinthians 12:7-10). All these "manifestations" of the Spirit he says are for the common good. They are given to enable the effective spiritual functioning of the Christian community.[4] We can see how these gifts like preaching and teaching are able to assist in the proclamation of the Gospel. In other words, St Paul recognises that some members of the Christian community may receive spiritual gifts precisely to enable the effective proclamation of the Christian message.

Some of these gifts propose that individual members of the Christian community may possess quite extraordinary spiritual capacities. Some may be able to prophesise, some to heal the sick, some to work miracles. This list suggests that the Christian community in Corinth witnessed the presence of these gifts. St Paul was simply explaining what the purposes of God were in bestowing these gifts on individuals. This passage encourages us not to discount extraordinary manifestations of the Spirit among Christians. The purpose of the manifestation of such gifts, we note, is linked to task of evangelisation. Such gifts rightly exercised can be powerful means

---

4 See 1 Corinthians 12:4-7: "Now there are varieties of gifts, but the same Spirit; and there are varieties of service, but the same Lord; and there are varieties of working, but it is the same God who inspires them all in every one. To each is given the manifestation of the Spirit for the common good."

of giving witness to the truth and power of the Christian message. The history of the Church witnesses to the presence of such gifts. One can think of miracles associated with the preaching of great saints like St Anthony of Padua.[5] The healings that have occurred at the Marian shrine at Lourdes have brought many to the faith.[6]

In a section of his letter to the Galatians, St Paul speaks of the action of the Holy Spirit in the life of the believer. Contrasting the effects of the Spirit with the effects of living a self-indulgent life, St Paul lists what he calls the "fruits of the Spirit". He mentions love, joy, peace, patience, kindness, goodness, faithfulness, gentleness and self-control (Galatians 2:22). St Paul, again speaking from his experience, sees that a person who has opened their life to the Spirit can experience real ways in which the Spirit transforms their character. Particular virtues become evident in the life of the Christian. Under the influence of the Spirit the character of the Christian is transformed to be more like Christ. The presence of these fruits of the Spirit in the life of

---

5 St Anthony of Padua is one of the most famous disciples of St Francis of Assisi. He was a famous preacher and worker of miracles. The number of those who came to hear him was sometimes so great that no church was large enough to accommodate and so he had to preach in the open air. Frequently St. Anthony wrought miracles of conversion. Mutual enemies were reconciled with one another. Thieves were converted and made restitution. His enemies and enemies of the Church were moved to recant. He was so energetic in defending the truths of the Catholic Faith that many heretics returned to the Church.

6 Sixty-eight miracles have been officially recognised as having occurred at Lourdes. There is the celebrated case of Dr Alexis Carrel (1873-1944), French surgeon, biologist and sociologist, who personally witnessed a miracle at Lourdes and wrote in a book, "If God exists, miracles are possible. But does God exist objectively? Does the Virgin exist outside our own minds? How am I to know? ... To convince me that miracles exist, I would have to see an organic disease cured, a leg growing back after amputation, a cancer disappearing, a congenital dislocation suddenly vanishing. If such things could be scientifically proved then it would be permissible to admit the intervention of a supernatural power." Visiting Lourdes he found himself praying, "Gentle Virgin who brings help to the unfortunate who humbly implore you, keep me with you. I believe in you. You did answer my prayers by a blazing miracle."

the Christian enables the Christian to be a credible witness to Christ in the world.

A person who lives a life under the influence of the Holy Spirit grows in virtues that are very attractive. Some people are drawn to Christianity because they sense that the Christian has something extra in their lives. It was not the oratorical skills of St Ambrose of Milan that attracted the great thinker Augustine, but the sense that St Ambrose had something Augustine lacked. It was his encounter with St Ambrose that led Augustine down the track to conversion and baptism by the great bishop of Milan.[7]

The Holy Spirit is an invisible yet real presence in the Church and in the Christian life. The Spirit's activity is recognised in spiritual gifts which give the Christian capacity to be transformed and empowered to give witness before the world of a new reality possible for human life. The activity of the Holy Spirit in the life of the Christian is oriented towards the work of evangelisation. These gifts are given not just for the personal benefit of the individual but for the mission of the Church.

Spirit as breath

In St John's account of the first appearance of the risen Lord to his disciples on Easter Sunday evening, we are told that Jesus "breathed on them" and said, "Receive the Holy Spirit" (John 20:22). The action of breathing is worth noting. It is actually the same word as the word for wind, in Hebrew, *ruah*.

---

[7] Augustine was attracted by the preaching of St Ambrose of Milan, not so much with an expectation of profiting spiritually by it as to examine the quality of his eloquence. He found the discourses were more learned than the heresies he had adopted, and began to read the New Testament, especially Saint Paul's writings. This would eventually lead to his conversion.

This tells us something very important about the role of the Holy Spirit and personal faith. Without breath we have no life. Every moment of our lives we are breathing in and out. It goes on so consistently that we do not notice, except when we run or exert ourselves and are gasping for breath. The Spirit of God breathes in us. While we are usually not conscious of his activity the Holy Spirit is at work within us. It is steady and life-giving. For instance, St Paul teaches that we could not have faith but that the Spirit moves in us (1 Corinthians 12:3). We are brought to and sustained in our faith by the movement of the Holy Spirit within us.

This link between faith and the Holy Spirit is very important when we come to consider evangelisation. In the work of evangelisation it is the action of the Holy Spirit which enables a person to come to faith. It is the Holy Spirit that enables a person to grow in faith. The evangelist must learn to evangelise "in the Spirit".

Evangelisation, in the end, is not a human activity. The preacher is simply an instrument of the Holy Spirit. Evangelisation is essentially a spiritual activity.

Traditionally in Catholic theology we speak of sanctifying grace and actual grace. Actual grace can be described in terms of various particular gifts of the Spirit, while sanctifying grace refers to the abiding presence of the Holy Spirit. Sanctifying grace, then, could be described using the image of breath, as the Spirit breathing within us. This "breathing" is the ground to our faith. It is the basis upon which other particular actions of the Spirit can occur.

Spirit as Fire

The other sign that accompanied the coming of the Spirit upon the disciples was the tongues of fire that hovered over each of them. It is as though God declared, "I am going to light a fire in the hearts of the disciples." The power of the Spirit was to burn away all fear and hesitancy. It was to make them strong and confident. They were to be "on fire" with zeal for the Gospel.

Jesus had said at an earlier time, "I came to cast fire upon the earth; and would that it were already kindled" (Luke 12:49). Jesus himself manifested a character that, while able to be deeply compassionate, was bold and courageous. He was strong and definite in his teaching and his actions. He knew his teaching would upset people, but he was undaunted.[8] His disciples needed to have the same courage and zeal.

There is no doubt that the power of the Holy Spirit inspired the Apostles to engage in the great work of evangelisation. They would carry the Gospel to the ends of the earth as known at that time. St Peter moved to Rome to be at the heart of the world of his day. St Paul travelled across the Mediterranean world. St Thomas went to India. St Mark evangelised in Alexandria. The Great Commission was being fulfilled – the disciples, even in the first years of fulfilling their mission, were going to the ends of the earth.

Not only did they become bold and courageous preachers of Jesus Christ, but all, except John, would suffer a martyr's death: such was their ultimate witness to Christ. They would give their lives for him. There was a fire in their hearts.

Evangelisation cannot be carried out in some kind of dispassionate way. It is a provocative and challenging message of the truth about human life and the action of God to redeem humanity. An evangelist is one whose heart is on fire. The Holy Spirit gives the words that can touch hearts.

---

8 The cleansing of the Temple is one dramatic example of bold action by Christ. It is recorded in all four Gospels. The account occurs near the end of the Synoptic Gospels (Mark 11:15-19, 11:27-33, Matthew 21:12-17, 21:23-27 and Luke 19:45-48, 20:1-8) and near the start in the Gospel of John (John 2:13-16).

Principal agent of evangelisation

In a general audience on 30 November 1972 Pope Paul VI commented: "On several occasions we have asked about the greatest needs of the Church." He responds to his question in these words: "We must say it, almost trembling and praying, because as you know well, this is the Church's mystery and life: the Spirit, the Holy Spirit." His declaration is clear and bold – the greatest need of the Church is the Holy Spirit.

The Pope describes what the Spirit does in the Church in these stirring and poetic words:

> He it is who animates and sanctifies the Church. He is her divine breath, the wind in her sails, the principle of her unity, the inner source of her light and strength. He is her support and consoler, her source of charisms and songs, her peace and her joy, her pledge and prelude to blessed and eternal life.

He then adds: "The Church needs her perennial Pentecost; she needs fire in her heart, words on her lips, prophesy in her outlook. She needs to be a temple of the Holy Spirit." Pope Paul turned longingly to God praying for the gift of the Holy Spirit to be poured out afresh in his day. Such an outpouring he knew would animate the Church and enable it to be spiritually alive and evangelically effective.

After reading these words it is not hard to understand why the Pope devoted special attention to the role of the Holy Spirit in the work of evangelisation in his great Apostolic Exhortation on evangelisation in the modern world, *Evangelii Nuntiandi*.⁹ Pope Paul had the deep conviction that "evangelisation will never be possible without the action of the Holy Spirit". He describes the indispensable role of the Holy Spirit in the evangelisation enterprise in these words:

> The Holy Spirit is the soul of the Church. It is He who explains to the faithful the deep meaning of the teaching of Jesus and of His mystery. It is the Holy Spirit who, today just as at the beginning of the Church, acts in every evangeliser who allows himself to be possessed and led by Him. The Holy Spirit places on his lips the words which he could not find by himself, and at the same time the Holy Spirit predisposes the soul of the hearer to be open and receptive to the Good News and to the kingdom being proclaimed. Techniques of evangelization are good, but even the most advanced ones could not replace the gentle action of the Spirit. The most perfect preparation of the evangeliser has no effect without the Holy Spirit. Without the Holy Spirit the most convincing dialectic has no power over the heart of man. Without Him the most highly developed schemas resting on a sociological or psychological basis are quickly seen to be quite valueless.[10]

It is quite clear that Pope Paul sees the Holy Spirit as indispensable to the work of evangelisation. He describes the Holy Spirit as the "principal agent of evangelisation". He says, "It is He who impels

---

9 *Evangelii Nuntiandi* was issued on 8 December 1975 by Pope Paul VI following the work of the synod on the theme which met in Rome September/October 1974. It derives its name from the first words of the text: Evangelii nuntiandi studium nostrae aetatis hominibus (The effort to proclaim the Gospel to the men of our time). This apostolic exhortation to new missionary fervour gave a new impetus to the Church, and inspired the teaching of John Paul II who participated heavily in its drafting.
10 *Evangelii Nuntiandi*, n. 75.

each individual to proclaim the Gospel, and it is He who in the depths of consciences causes the word of salvation to be accepted and understood." Finally, in this section of *Evangelii Nuntiandi*, Pope Paul comments very simply and yet with prophetic insight: "We live in the Church at a privileged moment of the Spirit." He then refers to the many religious orders who have contributed to the missionary endeavour of the Church, but one senses he is aware that a new missionary thrust is about to occur, one that will be occasioned by the sovereign action of the Holy Spirit.

The Pope, while acknowledging the work of evangelisation accomplished in past times, looks to a fresh movement of the Holy Spirit to inspire a new generation of evangelisers. He is absolutely convinced that the principal agent of evangelisation is not us, but the Holy Spirit. Evangelisation, he says "will never be possible without the action of the Holy Spirit".

In his lengthy treatment of the place of the Holy Spirit in the evangelising mission of the Church the Pope explores the vital role of the Spirit in the life and mission of Jesus. The public ministry of Jesus began with the power of the Spirit coming upon him at his baptism. He notes that Jesus was "led by the Spirit" to the desert and then "in the power of the Spirit" he returned to Galilee and commenced his mission. The Spirit was an active presence and guide in his ministry. Pope Paul notes that after his Resurrection as he was about to send out his disciples he says, breathing on them, "Receive the Holy Spirit." The Apostles will go out in the power of the Spirit. This was realised particularly at Pentecost.

Pope Paul speaks of the Holy Spirit as the key agent which generates the inner life of the Church and the Holy Spirit is the principal means by which the mission of the Church can be realised. In speaking of the first preaching of the Gospel by St Peter on Pentecost day he says,

"Peter is filled with the Holy Spirit so that he can speak to the people about Jesus, the Son of God." The preaching of St Paul is inspired by the Spirit and he adds, "The Spirit, who causes Peter, Paul and the Twelve to speak, and who inspires the words that they are to utter, also comes down on those who heard the word." The Spirit not only inspires the preacher but moves in the heart of the hearer.

The Pope describes the Spirit as the "soul of the Church". The Pope reminds us that when we look at the Church it is not the exterior life or activities that are finally important. What is important is the quality of its inner life. Quoting St Luke he is aware that it is in the "consolation of the Holy Spirit" that the Church increases. In the mind of the Pope there is no doubt that the work of the Holy Spirit is of vital importance in the evangelising process.

When the evangeliser understands that the Holy Spirit is the key agent in evangelisation then a correct perspective is given to the role of methods and programmes. The Pope comments that it is not simply a question of the refining of various techniques and methods. Methods and techniques are necessary but we must not rely upon them alone. It is not the skill with which we go about the evangelising work, but our humble reliance on the Holy Spirit. Nothing can replace the action of the Holy Spirit. This is of vital importance when considering the work of evangelisation. Thus, it will be the dispositions in the heart of the evangeliser that are of most importance. While techniques and methods need to be developed, the Pope warns that fruitfulness will be the result ultimately of the fact that these means are merely the vehicles for the working of the Spirit.

Pope Paul is hopeful and confident that a new era in evangelisation is upon us when he commented that he believed that we are living at "a privileged moment of the Spirit".

He concludes his comments in paragraph 75 of *Evangelii Nuntiandi* by saying:

> It must be said that the Holy Spirit is the principal agent of evangelisation: it is He who impels each individual to proclaim the Gospel, and it is He who in the depths of consciences causes the word of salvation to be accepted and understood. But it can equally be said that He is the goal of evangelisation: He alone stirs up the new creation, the new humanity of which evangelisation is to be the result, with that unity in variety which evangelisation wishes to achieve within the Christian community.

While we are naturally drawn to consider the "how" of evangelisation we must never forget that in the end it is the work of God through the Holy Spirit. Truly fruitful evangelisation will not be the result of the skill or effort that we give to it. At the same time God needs us – our dedication, our initiative, our service – so that evangelisation can take place.

Evangelisation began with the outpouring of the Holy Spirit at Pentecost and it will continue in the Church through the sovereign action of the Holy Spirit.

2

The Message: Preaching the Crucified Christ

The first proclamation of the Christian Gospel by St Peter made the declaration that Jesus of Nazareth who was crucified had risen from the dead: "Let all the house of Israel therefore know assuredly that God has made him both Lord and Christ, this Jesus whom you crucified" (Acts 2:36). The Church proclaimed that Jesus Christ had risen from the dead and announced the significance of his death and resurrection. Jesus is Lord (a divine title)[11] and Messiah (the promised saviour of Israel).[12]

The focus of the preaching of the Church is upon Jesus. We announce the mystery of God's intervention in history and the resultant effect on human lives.

This can be compared with the preaching of Jesus himself. His message was: "The Kingdom of God is close at hand." In linking the message of Jesus with the message of the Church we could say that the Kingdom of God which was described by Jesus as being "close at hand" is now realised through the saving death and resurrection of

---

11 When the Hebrew Bible was translated into Greek (the Septuagint) the word *Kurios* – Lord – was used as the divine title for God.

12 The title Christ comes from the Greek *Christós* which means anointed. This word is a translation of the Hebrew Māšîaḥ, from which we have the word, Messiah. The New Testament proclaimed Jesus as the promised Messiah. The followers of Jesus became known as Christians (see Acts 11:36) because they believed Jesus to be the Christos (or Messiah). The Christian faith gave this name to Jesus of Nazareth thus proclaiming him as Jesus the Christ.

Jesus. The death and resurrection of Jesus effectively established the Kingdom of God.[13]

However, the key thrust of Christian preaching needs to be further teased out: what does the Church want to proclaim to the world? What is the precise content of our message? And, more importantly, how can we present a message that engages the minds and hearts of contemporary peoples? What does the Church have to offer to the world today?

The preaching of St Paul

The most developed "theology of Christian preaching" is found in the thought of St Paul. He was not only the great evangeliser but he reflected on his role and experience. Through his various encounters with both Jews and Gentiles he hammered out what was the key message that the Church was to preach. To him we can turn to understand the way in which the early Church proclaimed the message to the world.

St Paul was the great evangeliser. We imagine him as a bold and zealous preacher. And he was. However, in light of this impression of him consider his comments to the Corinthian community provided in his first letter to them. Recalling his first visit to their city he made some quite surprising remarks about his disposition of heart as he approached Corinth: "When I came to you, brethren, I did not come proclaiming to you the testimony of God in lofty words or wisdom" (1 Corinthians 2:1). He adds, "And I was with you in weakness and in

---

13 Jesus described Satan as having a kingdom in this world (see Matthew 12:26). In the third of the temptations Satan offers Jesus all the kingdoms of this world if he would bow down and worship him (see Luke 4:5-7). In the mind of Jesus Satan holds sway in this world and he has come to wrest control from Satan and bring in a new kingdom where God reigns in the hearts of people. See also Colossians 1:13.

much fear and trembling." This is a surprising admission; one that we would not have expected to hear from St Paul.

In order to understand what prompted these comments we need to consider his experiences before reaching Corinth. Prior to arriving in Corinth St Paul had been in Athens. Athens was not only the political capital of Greece, but it was the intellectual centre of Greek culture. Even though Rome was now the political power of the world of that time, Athens retained a pre-eminence as an intellectual centre. In the past it had produced the great philosophers – Socrates, Plato and Aristotle – and Greek philosophy continued to be a major intellectual influence in the world of Paul's time.

In the Acts of the Apostles, chapter 17, we read the account of St Paul's visit to the Areopagus.[14] St Luke describes St Paul's preaching is these words:

> Men of Athens, I perceive that in every way you are very religious. For as I passed along, and observed the objects of your worship, I found also an altar with this inscription, "To an unknown god." What therefore you worship as unknown, this I proclaim to you (Acts 17:22-23).

St Paul approached this crowd of thinkers by attempting to mount an argument for the existence of God. He sought to present the Gospel in philosophical terms. He hoped to appeal to their reason.

It appears that his preaching achieved little. No Christian community was established at that time it seems – we have no Letter to the Athenians. It appears St Paul left Athens after a short time. Again this suggests that he made little progress in this city of philosophers.

His first letter to the Corinthians describes his personal state as he walked on to Corinth. He was shaken by his experience in Athens.

---

14 The Areopagus, or "Hill of Ares" in Athens was the site of the meeting of the Council of Elders of the city.

He came down to the bustling port city with not a little "fear and trembling" (2:4). He had made an error in Athens in trying to present the Gospel in the terms of philosophy. This approach had not worked. So when he arrived in Corinth he had made up his mind as to how he would preach. He states: "For I decided to know nothing among you except Jesus Christ and him crucified" (1 Corinthians 2:2).

He goes on to add: "My speech and my message were not in plausible words of wisdom, but in demonstration of the Spirit and of power, that your faith might not rest in the wisdom of men but in the power of God."

Following this personal statement St Paul delivers his new grasp of what the message of Christianity must be:

> Yet among the mature we do impart wisdom, although it is not a wisdom of this age or of the rulers of this age, who are doomed to pass away. But we impart a secret and hidden wisdom of God, which God decreed before the ages for our glorification. None of the rulers of this age understood this; for if they had, they would not have crucified the Lord of glory (1 Corinthians 2:6-8).

As he continues his reflection on Christian preaching he says, "And we impart this in words not taught by human wisdom but taught by the Spirit, interpreting spiritual truths to those who possess the Spirit" (1 Corinthians 2:12-16). As he continues he comes to what he now clearly understands as the key to his preaching:

> For Jews demand signs and Greeks seek wisdom, but we preach Christ crucified, a stumbling block to Jews and folly to Gentiles, but to those who are called, both Jews and Greeks, Christ the power of God and the wisdom of God. For the foolishness of God is wiser than men, and the weakness of God is stronger than men (1 Corinthians 1:22-25).

Thus St Paul had resolved to do one thing and one thing only – to proclaim a crucified Christ. He knows that it is a stumbling block for the Jews and simple madness for the Greeks. However, he knows that it is in the cross that the power of God to save is revealed. So he is prepared to abandon human wisdom and embrace the "foolishness" of the message of the cross.

This is the key to the message that the Church has to offer to the world. Like St Paul we know it will be a stumbling block for many and we know we can look foolish in what we proclaim. However, we know that this is the truth of what God has done in and through his Son, Jesus Christ. God has acted to save humanity by means of a sacrificial death. Christian faith is about receiving and embracing this salvation.

The Church today proclaims this mystery of the crucified Christ. Of all the other proclamations and presentations that can make up the preaching of the Gospel, this truth must be central to what is proclaimed. St Paul knew that in a mysterious way proclaiming the crucified Christ released the power of God in people's lives. When a person is moved in the depth of their being by the realisation of the meaning of the death of Christ for them, then something happens within them. They are convicted of a profound truth that moves them to an acceptance of faith in Jesus Christ and a desire to live their lives in union with him.

The power of the cross in St John

St Paul became convinced that the key to preaching with power is to proclaim unambiguously the Cross of Christ. Let us consider this central focus of the preaching of the Gospel from another viewpoint – this time that of St John.

St John provides a unique account of the crucifixion because he was the only evangelist there. He provides some important material not given by other evangelists. His text alone records the piercing of the heart of Jesus.

It is something which St John realised was of great significance, as he commented in his Gospel account: "He who saw it has borne witness – his testimony is true, and he knows that he tells the truth – that you also may believe" (John 19:35). Here the issue for St John is not just the fact that the heart of Jesus was pierced by the soldier's lance, but the fact that blood and water flowed from his pierced side.

To understand the significance of the blood and water for St John it is necessary to consider some other Johannine passages.

In 1 John 5:5-8 he speaks of the "two witnesses"; those "witnesses" being the blood and the water. This was written by St John many years after the events of Calvary and one can see the clear reference to what he described in his Gospel.

What St John means by "witness" is that the blood and water which flowed from the heart of Jesus have symbolic meaning. Blood is seen as expressive of the sacrifice offered. This was the common Jewish understanding associated with the sacrifice of animals offered to God. Thus, for example, the blood of bulls was the sacrificial offering made to God at the time of the establishing of the Covenant at Sinai.[15] Jewish people made pilgrimages to Jerusalem to offer sacrifices to God. Thus, we see Mary and Joseph with their newborn going to Jerusalem to offer a sacrifice for their firstborn son.[16]

It is worth commenting at this point about a peculiarly Johannine reference where John the Baptist refers to Jesus as the "lamb of

---
15 See Exodus 29:12-22.
16 See Luke 2:22-24.

God".[17] This is seen as a description of Jesus as the sacrificial lamb – one who would offer himself up to God in a sacrificial death.

The other "witness" is water. Water here is a reference to the life-giving Spirit. Again the Johannine writings reveal a particular line of thought. In John 7:37-39 he writes:

> On the last day of the feast, the great day, Jesus stood up [in the temple] and proclaimed, "If any one thirst, let him come to me and drink. He who believes in me, as the scripture has said, 'Out of his heart shall flow rivers of living water.'"

St John then adds his own comment:

> Now this he said about the Spirit, which those who believed in him were to receive; for as yet the Spirit had not been given, because Jesus was not yet glorified.

Water, in the mind of St John, is equated with the Spirit which has not yet been sent because Jesus has not yet been glorified (that is, he had not yet died on the Cross). Thus, for St John, the death of Jesus on the cross was the sacrifice by which the Holy Spirit was to be released.

The full meaning of the death of Jesus became clearly evident as he witnessed the piercing of the heart of Jesus. It seems that when he saw the flowing forth of the last drops of blood and the release of the waters from the heart of Jesus that the evangelist, St John, had a moment of personal revelation. At that instant he realised the meaning of what he was witnessing. The death of Jesus was not just the tragic ending of his life. It was not just the achievement of the Chief Priests and Elders who sought to silence him. It was the means by which God redeemed humanity and released the power of the Holy Spirit.

---

17 See John 1:29.

St John concludes his account by quoting from Zechariah 12:10: "They shall look on him whom they have pierced" (John 19:37). As St John looked up at the cross and saw the pierced heart from which the blood and water flowed he came to understand the purposes of God. He is encouraging us to do the same. In his Gospel the idea is offered earlier. In John 3:13 the evangelist writes: "No-one has ascended into heaven but he who descended from heaven, the Son of man. And as Moses lifted up the serpent in the wilderness, so must the Son of man be lifted up." And also in John 8:28 St John records Jesus as saying in reference to being lifted up: "then you will know that I am he". In other words, Jesus is saying that his crucifixion will be the full revelation of who he is and what his life and mission were all about.

St John wants us to realise, as he came to realise, that this is how we are to know Jesus: as the crucified one. We are to contemplate him on the cross, particularly looking upon his pierced heart from which the blood and water flow. Thus we can come to see the full meaning of who Jesus is. We will not just know Jesus as a good man, the epitome of human virtue; or as a wise teacher who has given us a moral code; as one who exemplifies the ideals of love and compassion. We will come to know him in the fullness of his purpose.

We look to the crucified Christ and it is there that we find his deepest identity. Looking upon the crucified Christ we stand in awe before this revelation of the depth of his love and compassion for humanity. In the crucified Christ is found the salvation that God has won for us. Herein is the profound mystery of God. In the heart of Jesus pierced is the final and full revelation of the nature of God and what God has done for our sake.

St John, like St Paul, understands that the Christian Gospel is the proclamation of the Crucified Christ.

Preaching salvation in Jesus Christ

Pope Paul in his encyclical, *Evangelii Nuntiandi*, expressed the message of Christianity in these words:

> As the kernel and centre of His Good News, Christ proclaims salvation, this great gift of God which is liberation from everything that oppresses man but which is above all liberation from sin and the Evil One, in the joy of knowing God and being known by Him, of seeing Him, and of being given over to Him.[18]

The heart of the message that the Church proclaims to the world is the proclamation of Jesus Christ is the source of salvation. Pope Paul makes it abundantly clear:

> Evangelisation will also always contain – as the foundation, centre, and at the same time, summit of its dynamism – a clear proclamation that, in Jesus Christ, the Son of God made man, who died and rose from the dead, salvation is offered to all men, as a gift of God's grace and mercy.[19]

This is what the Church is to proclaim to the world. The Christian message is far more than the presentation of a personal morality. It is not simply an invitation to join the Church. It is not proposing some form of ethical consciousness. The Pope is clear: what we declare to the world is that Jesus Christ offers the path of salvation. In preaching Christ, we are not just preaching the person of Jesus, for instance, as the embodiment of certain virtues or attitudes.

While we look to the character of the Lord Jesus as revealed in the life and teaching of Jesus of Nazareth, it is not just his life, but rather his death that is the heart of our Christian proclamation.

---

18 *Evangelii Nuntiandi*, n. 9.
19 Ibid., n. 57.

In the Mass when we are asked to proclaim the mystery of faith we declare: "We proclaim your death O Lord." In the third of the options we declare Jesus as "Saviour of the world" because "by your Cross and Resurrection you have set us free". We proclaim the death of Christ as the key to the purposes of God in sending His Son as our redeemer.

This was a very important message for St Paul. After his experience in Athens where he tried to argue that Christ was the unknown God of the philosophers, he learnt that he needed to preach "a crucified Christ" (1 Corinthians 2:2). He realised that he needed to proclaim the "foolishness" of the cross, which, he realised, made no sense to those who looked for human wisdom. Similarly St John understood that in the piercing of the heart of Jesus we can understand that his death realised the outpouring of the life-giving Spirit.

The understanding of the significance of the cross that both St Paul and St John reached is the heart of the message that the Church is to proclaim in our time.

Preaching of St Peter

We have mentioned St Paul and St John. What about the preaching of St Peter? Does it accord with their focus?

The heart of the message of St Peter at Pentecost was, as we saw: "Let all the house of Israel therefore know assuredly that God has made him both Lord and Christ, this Jesus whom you crucified" (*Acts* 2:36). This declaration was followed by the invitation to his hearers to repent, to become disciples of Jesus by being baptised in his name for the forgiveness of sins, and thus to receive the gift of the Holy Spirit.[20]

---

20 See Acts 2:38.

St Peter understood that the Christian message was about salvation. When brought before the Sanhedrin to explain himself, St Peter provided this clarification of the centrality of preaching Jesus Christ: "And there is salvation in no-one else, for there is no other name under heaven given among men by which we must be saved" (Acts 4:12).

The experience St Peter had on the occasion of the conversion of the pagan Roman Cornelius was an important moment of confirmation of his message. It revealed to St Peter that Jesus was saviour of all, not just the Jews.[21] St Luke records that as St Peter preached "the Holy Spirit fell on all who heard the word". We are told that those who had accompanied Peter were astonished that "the gift of the Holy Spirit had been poured out even on the Gentiles" (Acts 10:44-45). Universal salvation in Jesus Christ was the message of the Church to the world.

A universal Gospel

The realisation that salvation was intended for all enabled the Church to break free from focusing on Jews alone and launched the apostolate to the Gentiles.

St Paul understood that the Gospel was intended for all. In his Letter to the Ephesians St Paul describes his own ministry as one of proclaiming to the Gentiles the "unfathomable treasure of Christ".[22]

The Apostles came to see that what was accomplished by Christ was the fulfillment of a plan "formed long ago" (Ephesians 3:9). They understood the sweep of history. They understood that God

---

21 See Acts 10:1-48. This account of the conversion of Cornelius is given in much detail because it demonstrates that the Gospel is equally intended for pagans as well as Jews.
22 See Ephesians 3:8-11.

"desires all men to be saved and to come to the knowledge of the truth. For there is one God, and there is one mediator between God and men, the man Christ Jesus, who gave himself as a ransom for all" (1 Timothy 2:4-6).

Witnesses to what God has done

St John speaks of his role as a witness to what God has done. He considers himself privileged to have seen Jesus and discovered his mystery (See John 13:23-25; 21:24). His writings reveal his enthusiasm to share what he has discovered: "that which we have seen and heard we proclaim to you, so that you may have fellowship with us; and our fellowship is with the Father and with his Son Jesus Christ" (1 John 1:3).

St John is able to see the whole mystery of Christ. He provides profound insight into the work of God in Christ. He provides a beautiful meditation on the Incarnation at the commencement of his Gospel: "And the Word became flesh and dwelt among us, full of grace and truth; we have beheld his glory, glory as of the only-begotten Son from the Father" (John 1:14).

St John knows that God is revealed in and through his Son.[23] Jesus is not only the revelation of the Father but the way to the Father. Jesus is the Way, the Truth and the Life (John 14:6). He is truly, as St John says, "the Saviour of the World" (John 4:42).

---

23 See John 14:9.

3

A Brief History of Evangelisation

The story of the Church is the account of the fulfilling of the Great Commission. Throughout the ages the task of evangelisation has been taken up by the Church. While there is evidence of a steady application to the task, it is possible to detect special moments where there have been surges in evangelising activity.

These surges can be listed as the initial surge in apostolic times; the post-Dark Ages surge headed by the monastic orders; the evangelical revival of the 13th century promoted by the friars (Franciscans and Dominicans particularly); the Counter Reformation surge spearheaded by the new apostolic clerical orders like the Jesuits; and the 19th century missionary endeavour taken up by various missionary congregations of priests, brothers and nuns.

History may well reveal that there was a surge at the beginning of the third Christian millennium as the Church responded to the call for a new evangelisation.

The initial surge in Apostolic times

The Acts of the Apostles is an account of the spread of the Church in its earliest years. The first expansion of Christianity was from Jerusalem to Caesarea and Joppa. From there, the message moved on to Samaria and Syria. The Apostle Paul carried out extensive missionary activity in Asia Minor and Greece. St Peter later moved to Rome, beginning the tradition of the Church being centred in that city rather than its origin in Jerusalem.

The first Christian work of evangelisation occurred among the Jews. It was Jewish pilgrims who heard the message at Pentecost. However the expansion of the Christian mission beyond Judaism – to the Gentiles – took place very early. The Apostle Paul was an early proponent of this expansion, and presented the Christian message to the Greek and Roman cultures, enabling it to reach beyond its Hebrew and Jewish origins. This was a significant development as evangelisation soon reached out to all Gentile nations. It was not long before Gentile Christians would outnumber Jewish Christians. In its early stages, though, this expansion was not without controversy. Some Jewish members of the newly emerging Church wanted to require acceptance of Jewish customs like circumcision as a prerequisite for entering the Christian faith. The first Council of the Church, held in Jerusalem, resolved that this was not a necessary requirement and so removed a possible obstacle to Gentiles embracing the Christian faith.

Early persecution of Christians in Jerusalem encouraged the spread of message. James, the brother of John, was the first Apostle to be martyred, about 44AD. Persecution has always accompanied the evangelising mission of the Church. The first Christians experienced it from their own Jewish compatriots and later centuries of intermittent and at times extremely harsh persecution came from the Roman authorities.

In the coming centuries Christianity spread throughout the Roman Empire. St Peter and St Paul both died as martyrs in Rome, but the task they began was continued by others. By the end of the first century, the Christian church had expanded widely across the Mediterranean world. Christianity crossed the Mediterranean from Italy into the Roman provinces in North Africa. It spread into

Egypt. Simultaneously, previous Christian gains were consolidated as Christianity spread from urban centres into the surrounding countryside.

Christianity was not confined to the boundaries of the Roman Empire. Tradition has it that the Apostle Thomas conducted missionary journeys into India, founding the Christian church there. According to Eusebius' record, the Apostles Thomas and Bartholomew were assigned to Parthia (modern Iran). By the time of the establishment of the Second Persian Empire (226AD), there were bishops of the Church of the East in northwest India, Afghanistan and Pakistan, with laymen and clergy alike engaging in missionary activity. By the third century, there were Christians in Arabia. The conversion of King Tiridates helped to bring the faith to Armenia.

During third century Christianity developed strongly in North Africa, which produced such Christian leaders as Cyprian, Tertullian, and Augustine. Carthage remained a strong centre for Christianity for centuries, until it was conquered by Islamic invaders in the early 700s. The Church in North Africa produced countless saints, martyrs and virgins.

The Church in Rome, closely associated with the Apostles Peter and Paul had become a focal point for Christianity by the third century, moving also into northern Italy. Gaul, modern France, received the faith through Greek colonists. Early Gallic centres of Christianity included Vienne and Lyons. By the third century, too, there was much Christian activity in Spain, particularly in the southern part of the country. Christianity was taken to Britain. By the end of the third century there was no part of the Roman Empire that had not been penetrated by Christianity.

Christianity was subject to periods of intense persecution until the Edict of Toleration of 311AD. Once toleration came, the Church rapidly established a visible presence as churches were able to be built, some under direct Roman patronage.

After the fall of the Roman Empire

Christianity had become closely tied to the Roman Empire established in Rome and in Byzantium. With the collapse of the Empire in Rome there was a period of social and religious dislocation. The monastic communities, particularly those established by St Benedict, played a key role in preserving Christian learning during this period. They kept alive craft and artistic skills while maintaining intellectual culture within their schools, scriptoria and libraries. They functioned as agricultural, economic and production centres as well as providing a focus for the spiritual life. In time they would become centres for evangelisation in the fifth and sixth centuries as monks went forth in missionary endeavours.

During this period the Visigoths and Lombards who had become tainted with the Arian heresy accepted Catholicism. Pope Gregory I – the first monk to become a pope – played a notable role in these conversions and dramatically reformed the ecclesiastical structures and administration which then launched renewed missionary efforts. He sent Augustine and a group of monks to Britain in 597AD.

In the eighth century the "apostle of the Germans", Boniface, an English Benedictine, went to preach to the Saxons in Germany. He received permission to undertake a mission to Friesland (now part of the Netherlands) in 716AD. Two years later he was in Rome, receiving papal approval to preach to the right of the Rhine. Germany was evangelised.

St Patrick evangelised Ireland in the late fourth century. The fifth century saw Ireland become a major missionary church sending out monks to Scotland, England and France. The Irish monks had developed a concept of *peregrinatio*. This meant that a monk would leave the monastery and his own country to preach among the heathens. Soon Irish missionaries such as Columba and Columbanus spread Christianity, with its distinctively Irish features, to Scotland and the continent. From 590AD onwards Irish missionaries were an active evangelising presence in the Church and planted the faith in northern Britain and in Western Gaul.

At the end of the fifth century Clovis, king of the Franks, was baptised. The Franks were of Germanic origin and were part of the barbarian invasion which led to the fall of the Roman Empire. This baptism ushered in the evangelisation of the barbarian nations.

Christianity experienced a serious setback in its spread across the known world with the rise of Islam. In 610AD Muhammad claimed that he received revelations from God that called him to preach a new religion called Islam. At first he began to do so secretly, but after three years he found the courage to proclaim his new faith publicly and gained a growing number of followers.

Islam was able to spread by military conquest across northern Africa, and eastward into India. It captured the great Christian centres like Jerusalem, Alexandria and Carthage. Muslim missionary activity was fundamentally different from that of the Christians who preached a God of love. Muhammad taught that "Allah loves not those who reject Faith." It had spread through most of Spain by the early part of the eight century. In the east Constantinople held out preserving its Christian heritage, but it too fell to Islam in 1453.

The ninth, 10th and 11th centuries was the era during which the Christianity of Britain, of the Frankish Kingdom, and of Byzantium spread to encompass not only Scandinavia but also the predominantly Slavic peoples of central Europe and the Balkan Peninsula. Sweden became thoroughly Christianised in the 12th century, the last nation to be brought into the Frankish-Byzantine Christendom of Europe.

The great missionary achievement of the ninth century, however, was the conversion to Christianity of the Bulgarian and Moravian kings. The most notable extension of Byzantine Christianity during the 10th and early 11th centuries came about with the conversion of the Russian nation, centred in the province of Kiev. Poland was evangelised in the 10th century.

In *Ecclesia in Europa*, Pope John Paul II states:

> There can be no doubt that, in Europe's complex history, Christianity has been a central and defining element, established on the firm foundation of the classical heritage and the multiple contributions of the various ethnic and cultural steams which have succeeded one another down the centuries. The Christian faith has shaped the culture of the Continent and is inextricably bound up with its history, to the extent that Europe's history would be incomprehensible without reference to the events which marked first the great period of evangelisation and then the long centuries when Christianity, despite the painful division between East and West, came to be the religion of the European peoples.[24]

An evangelical revival

The Church in the 12th and 13th centuries began to experience an erosion of its spiritual role in Europe due to the rise of a variety of heretical sects. Knowledge and practice of the faith was at a low ebb and provided easy access for various heretical movements. The Church faced serious challenges as these heretical sects began to win adherents.

---

24 *Ecclesia in Europa*, n. 24.

The emergence of the Franciscans and Dominicans committed to a radical evangelical life and to the preaching of the basic Gospel message provided new spiritual energy for the Church. The Franciscans and Dominicans were at the forefront of missionary activity in the centuries that followed particularly as Europe discovered the Americas and the Far East.

New Worlds

The Age of Discovery inspired by European expansion into the Americas and then South East Asia opened up a new era of evangelisation.

Spanish Missions were established in the Americas as part of the Spanish colonisation of the New World. Beginning in 1493, the Kingdom of Spain established and maintained a number of missions throughout Nueva España (New Spain), consisting of Mexico and portions of what today are the southwestern parts of the United States in order to facilitate colonisation of these lands.

During this period the Church inaugurated a major effort to spread Christianity in the New World and to convert the indigenous peoples. The missionary effort was directly connected to the colonial efforts of European powers such as Spain, France and Portugal. The opening up of new areas of missionary activity coincided with the new energy in the Church coming from the Counter Reformation.

As Portugal and Spain opened up vast colonies in South America in the 1500s, missionaries accompanied the explorers and traders. Portugal concentrated on Eastern South America and the largest settlements were in Brazil, now the most populous Catholic country in the world. Spain concentrated on Western coast and located its primary centre in Peru.

Spanish missionaries penetrated into modern Mexico and southern United States. Evangelisation of the native populations was slow until the apparition of the Blessed Virgin to Juan Diego in 1531. The image of the Virgin imprinted on his tilba was indigenous in appearance with a dark complexion and a belt worn by pregnant local women around her waist. Our Lady of Guadalupe brought nine million Native Indians into the Church: the greatest single evangelising event ever.

In 1687, a Jesuit missionary named Father Eusebio Francisco Kino lived and worked with the native Americans in the area called the Pimería Alta which presently is located in the areas between the Mexican state of Sonora and the state of Arizona in the United States. During Father Eusebio Kino's stay in the Pimería Alta, he founded over 20 missions in eight mission districts.

Beginning in the second half of the 16th century, the Kingdom of Spain established a number of missions throughout Florida in order to convert the Indians to Christianity. In the Las Californias Province of New Spain in the Americas, Franciscans established and maintained missions from 1769 to 1823 for the purpose of converting the Native Americans. Junípero Serra, the Franciscan priest in charge of this effort, founded a series of mission outposts from San Diego to San Francisco Bay.

The French claimed eastern Canada, explored the St Lawrence River, the Great Lakes and the Mississippi and Ohio river valleys. The first Catholic missionaries in Canada were Recollects, who arrived in the first part of the 17th century. They were soon followed by Jesuits. Notable of these Jesuits were Jerome Lalemant, Jean de Brébeuf, and Isaac Jogues. They opened up the exploration of Canada and the upper Mississippi as they sought out native Indian tribes to convert to Catholicism.

Evangelisation of China

Contacts between the Mongols and the West occurred in the 13th century, as the Mongol Empire expanded towards Europe and Palestine, coinciding with the latter part of the Crusades. In 1253, King Louis IX sent the Franciscan William of Rubruck to the Mongol capital of Karakorum to convert the Tartars. In 1289, Pope Nicholas IV sent the Franciscan John of Monte Corvino to China by way of India. Friar John was China's first Catholic missionary, and he was significantly successful. He laboured largely in the Mongol tongue, translated the New Testament and Psalms, built a central church, and within a few years (by 1305) could report 6,000 baptised converts. However, the overthrow of the Mongol Yuan Dynasty by the Ming in 1368 resulted in forcing out foreign influences. By the 16th century, there is no reliable information about any practicing Christians remaining in China.

The missionary efforts and other work of the Society of Jesus between the 16th and 17th centuries played a significant role in re-establishing contact and the transmission of knowledge, science, and culture between China and the West. Members of the Jesuit delegation to China were perhaps the most influential of the different Christian missionaries in that country between the earliest period of the religion up until the 19th century, when significant numbers of Catholic and Protestant missions developed.

Prominent Jesuit missionaries included the Italian Matteo Ricci. At the time of their peak influence, members of the Jesuit delegation were considered some of the emperor's most valued and trusted advisers, holding numerous prestigious posts in the imperial government. When Ricci died in 1610 in Beijing, more than two thousand Chinese from all levels of society had confessed their faith in Jesus Christ.

However, between the 18th and mid-19th centuries, nearly all Western missionaries in China were forced to conduct their teaching and other activities covertly.

The great era of Western influence in China began in the mid-19th century as Western presence made itself felt in China. Over time the freedom for foreigners to evangelise and for Chinese to practice the Christian religion became part of the treaty system that came to define China's relations with the Western world. Meanwhile, the Christianisation of China once exclusively the province of the Catholic Church now became increasingly a Protestant undertaking, first dominated by the British but, later, overwhelmingly by Americans. This reflected the relative decline of the older Catholic powers in world affairs, Britain's leading role among Western nations in China, and the various energetic movements among English-speaking Protestants throughout the 19th century.

In the mid-19th century a pseudo-Christian movement called Taiping ("great peace") rose up against the ruling Manchu/Confucian dynasty. It was suppressed but did great damage to the standing of Christianity in China. The Boxer Uprising of 1900 violently attacked foreigners, Western Christians and, especially, Chinese Christians.

Christianity, in its American Protestant variant, contributed much to the secular modernisation of China. It was associated with the dominant reformist idea of the time, the social gospel, and its effects on Chinese society were profound. It was a powerful force in education, medicine, women's rights, and, especially, in introducing younger Chinese to the world through educational experiences in the United States.

The victory of Mao Zedong (1893-1976) and Communism meant once again that Christianity was persecuted in China. After Mao's death, China sought a "socialism with Chinese characteristics", as the late Deng Xiaoping named it, though in practice it resembles in many respects the kind of capitalism practiced by China's East Asian neighbours. The material advance of China and the dissociation with Buddhism under Communism has meant that China is spiritually thirsty.

The regime now recognises that its own de facto "edict of toleration", dating from the late 1970s, has allowed for an upsurge in Christian adherents, though we do not know how many. The regime itself uses a figure of about 10 million – six million Protestants and four million Catholics – but the real number is certainly higher. There is, likewise, a range of church-state relations, from furtive underground congregations harassed and hounded, to officially sanctioned "patriotic" churches and church organisations. The People's Republic and the Papacy, especially, have been locked in a 50-year struggle over the Communists' refusal to acknowledge the Vatican's right to name China's bishops.

Evangelisation in South East Asia

In the 16th century the evangelisation of Asia was linked initially to the Portuguese colonial policy. With the Papal bull Romanus Pontifex the patronage for the propagation of the Christian faith in Asia was given to the Portuguese. The Portuguese trade with Asia was profitable and as Jesuits came to India around 1540, the colonial government in Goa supported the mission with incentives for baptised Christians. Later, Jesuits were sent to China and further countries in Asia. With the decline of the Portuguese power, other colonial powers and Christian organisations gained influence. St Francis Xavier arrived in Goa in 1542. He preached down the coast of India. He went to Sri Lanka and the Moluccas, now part of Indonesia. He visited the Philippines and Japan. Although ill, he baptised thousands and died while waiting to enter China.

St Francis Xavier, fascinated by what he had heard of Japan made his way there in 1549. His evangelising efforts were slow but Christian communities developed. Nagasaki became a strong Christian centre. The growing presence of Christians eventually led to persecution in which thousands were martyred. Eventually all foreigners were expelled. After two and half centuries of absence in the 1850s European gunboats forced Japan to open up to foreigners. Missionaries arrived and were surprised to discover pockets of Catholics in Nagasaki. Evangelisation was slow and, following World War II, continued to progress slowly.

The history of Catholicism in Korea began in 1784 when Yi Sung-hun was baptised while in China under the Christian name of Peter. He later returned home with various religious texts and baptised many of his fellow countrymen. The Church in Korea survived without any formal missionary priests until clergy from France (the Paris Foreign Missions Society) arrived in 1836 for the ministry. Persecution of Catholics in the early days was ferocious with 8,000 being killed on a single occasion.

The Paris Foreign Mission Society, established in 1658, was an organisation of diocesan priests and lay people dedicated to the foreign mission. In the 350 years of its existence it has sent out 4,200 missionaries. A good deal of their effort was directed to Asia particularly in areas where there was a French trading presence. Missionaries went to Siam, Tonkin, Cochinchina and southern China. Their efforts extended to Laos and Cambodia. More than 40,000 people were baptised within a relatively short space of time. During the 19th century, the Catholic Church suffered persecution in these mission lands and produced thousands of martyrs.

Through French interests in Vietnam, the Catholic faith was implanted there. Early Catholics experienced intense persecution, with thousands being martyred in a 50 year period from 1820. When the French were driven out after World War II there were some three million Catholics mainly in the south of the country.

The most Catholic country in Asia is the Philippines. The Spanish occupied the Philippines in the mid-16th century in much the same way as they did countries in South America. Their presence led to the evangelisation of the people and the Catholicism was marked by deep personal piety. The Spanish were ousted by the Americans in 1898 but the faith was strongly established.

The spread of the Church to Indochina follows a similar pattern. In the 16th century the first missionary endeavours resulted in early converts, but then there was an extended period of often brutal persecution. Then a second wave of evangelisers, coming in the 19th century with the European expansion, was able to enter the country resulting in the establishment of a stable Catholic presence.

Today, Christianity is the predominant faith in the Philippines and East Timor. In South Korea, while the largest proportion of the population is irreligious, Christianity represents the most widespread religion, closely followed by Buddhism. Other countries have a small but vibrant Christian presence.

Africa

North Africa was one of the strongholds of early Christianity, but since the Muslim domination the Christian church has been almost non-existent. We can identify three phases of missionary effort in Africa. The first centuries of Christianity saw the evangelisation of Egypt and North Africa. There was a second phase involving the parts of the continent south of the Sahara, which took place in the 15th and 16th centuries. Then there was a third phase marked by an extraordinary missionary effort which began in the 19th century, the fruit of which is clearly in evidence today.

Churches, not at present in full communion with the Catholic Church – like the Greek Church of the Patriarchate of Alexandria, the Coptic Church of Egypt and the Church of Ethiopia – also advanced the mission of evangelisation often under very difficult conditions spreading south from Egypt.

In the 15th and 16th centuries, the exploration of the African coast by the Portuguese was soon accompanied by the evangelisation of the regions of Sub-Saharan Africa. That endeavour included the regions of present-day Benin, Angola, Mozambique and Madagascar. A certain number of Episcopal Sees were erected during this period, and one of the first fruits of that missionary endeavour was the consecration in Rome, by Pope Leo X in 1518, of Don Henrique, the son of Don Alfonso I, King of the Congo, as Titular Bishop of Utica. Don Henrique thus became the first native Bishop in Black Africa.

It was during this period, in 1622, that Pope Gregory XV permanently erected the Congregation de Propaganda Fide for the purpose of better organising and expanding the missionary work of the Church.

Because of various difficulties, the second phase of the evangelisation of Africa came to an end in the 18th century, with the disappearance of practically all the missions south of the Sahara.

However a new phase of evangelisation began in the 19th century, a period marked by an extraordinary effort organised by the great apostles and promoters of the African mission. Indeed, the growth of the Church in Africa over the last hundred years has been an extraordinary phenomenon.

Oceania

As early as the 16th century, when foreign missionaries first reached Oceania, island peoples heard and accepted the Gospel of Jesus Christ.

In 1836 Pope Gregory XVI commissioned the newly formed Society of Mary (Marist Fathers)[25] to bring Christianity to the Western Pacific. The first missionaries left in December that year. Outstanding among these evangelisers was St Peter Chanel martyred in 1841 on the island of Futuna. The Marists worked on Wallis Island (1837), Tonga (1842), New Caledonia (1843), Fiji (1844) and Samoa in 1845. The Marists under Bishop Pompallier established themselves in New Zealand in 1838 and set about the conversion of the Maori.

Though Protestant missionaries had often preceded them, the Marists established viable Catholic communities on many of the Pacific Islands and continued to serve these communities until relatively recent times when local clergy took up their work.

Missionary spring

In the 19th century the Catholic Church experienced a "missionary spring". While the Church in Europe was engaged in a struggle with modernity a new missionary impetus occurred as Catholic missionaries in their thousands reached out to the newly discovered peoples of Africa, Oceania, Asia and the Americas. This missionary spring came at a time when the European powers were expanding their influence into Asia, Africa and Oceania.

---

25 The Society of Mary was founded by the later ordained Fr Jean Claude Colin and other seminarians in 1816 in Lyon, France, and received approbation from the Holy See in 1836 to undertake the evangelisation of the Vicariate Apostolic of Western Oceania.

The result was the establishing of the Church in many of these nations. This missionary spirit stood in stark contrast to the great threat to traditional Catholicism by the rise of liberal states in Europe. The Church was traditionally wedded to political and social institutions of the old order and so was on the back foot. Yet a new surge of evangelising fervour flowed through the Church in countries like France, Spain, Italy, Germany and Holland.

This missionary expansion provided a means to rejuvenate the Church at a time when it was struggling to come to term with new political and social forces. The missionaries were fired by an evangelical zeal. Fr Daniele Comboni, now canonised, who founded African missions in the Sudan, said that missions "must be Catholic, not Spanish, or French, or German, or Italian". The missionaries felt that they were sons and defenders of a Church that was being persecuted and kept on the defensive by the rise of liberalism and the occurrence of a number of national revolutions. They saw the dangers in the political ideas of the 19th century and took on a spirit of what could be called "Catholic universalism".

Mission ad gentes today

The missionary task to take the Gospel to the ends of the earth still remains relevant for today. China is the great new missionary field. India also offers much possibility. Parts of Africa still need to be penetrated by the Gospel.

The great challenge for the Church at the present time is the rise of militant Islam. It strongly resists Christianity which it associates with Western culture. Many Christian communities which have origins back to Apostolic times are now experiencing serious threat which could result in these communities being driven out of a number of

Middle Eastern countries. In Africa, Islam is spreading southwards and threatens Christian communities in countries like Nigeria.

A great challenge for the evangelising mission of the Church is how it can undertake the conversion of Muslims.

4

The New Cultural Landscape

The Church has never forgotten the admonition of the Lord as he was about to ascend to the Father. As we have seen the Church has taken the Gospel message to the ends of the earth. Today Christianity is the largest single religion on earth and the Catholic Church is by far the largest Christian Church.

There still remain parts of the globe where the Gospel is still to be presented to peoples who have never heard of Christ. However, the Church faces new challenges in nations and cultures where it has been established sometimes for millennia. There are cultural factors at work which are weakening the faith of baptised Catholics and even drawing them out of the Church.

The cultural landscape is changing and the evangelising mission of the Church needs to be adapted to new challenges. In this chapter we will explore some of the key dimensions to the new cultural landscape emerging across the world. We will focus our attention more particularly on its expression in Australia.

Post-Conciliar generations
For the sake of identifying change we will use the time of the Second Vatican Council as a watershed moment. The Council has had a significant impact on Catholic life. The Council, held in the early

1960s, took place at a time when there was a period of significant social upheaval. The sexual revolution, university unrest, anti-war movements, drug culture and feminism were just some of the elements of social change in the West.

We will examine the changing situation of three generations after the Council. These generations were influenced by the changed face of the Church as a result of the Council. They were generations who lived through a time of significant social change.

For our purposes we can identify three generations – the Baby Boomers, Generation X and Generation Y. The Baby Boomers were born in the years following World War II and through their teenage years were influenced by the social turmoil of the 60s. Generation X are the children of the Baby boomers and were born in the 70s and 80s. Generation Y have grown up through the 1990s and into the new millennium.

To appreciate changes in Catholic life over this period it may be useful to paint a picture of Catholic life prior to the post-conciliar period. This will assist us in appreciating the vast changes that have come upon Catholic culture.

The Baby Boomer generation grew up at a time where Catholic identity was clearly defined. Family life in pre-television days more readily reflected Catholic practices. Grace was said before the family meal. Family prayer, perhaps a daily family rosary, was accepted as part of being a Catholic family. It was not unusual to see various Catholic symbols in the home – a statue of the Blessed Virgin Mary or a framed holy picture of the Sacred Heart or a saint on the wall. Many families were consecrated to the Sacred Heart of Jesus and a certificate recognised this. For those entering the house there were clear signs that this was a Catholic home.

A practising Catholic family was closely allied to the local parish. The religious life of the parish was not limited to Mass alone. There were various devotional activities, like Benediction on Sunday night and the Novena to Our Lady of Perpetual Succour during the week. Family members belonged to various sodalities – the Holy Name Society for men, the Sacred Heart Sodality for women, the Children of Mary for girls. Various societies were active in the parish, like the St Vincent de Paul Society and the Catholic Women's League.

Parish life offered not only a variety of religious events but also offered various social opportunities. There were the inevitable fundraising nights, Housie and fetes. The Catholic Youth Organisation held regular social events like dances and picnics, and offered a range of sporting activities. A Catholic could be a member of various Catholic associations, like a Catholic tennis club or the Catholic bushwalking club.

The presence of Religious in many parishes was very important. They were there because they staffed the parish primary or secondary school. The sisters and the brothers were a vital part of parish life. They were visibly present at major parish events. They often provided services beyond what they offered to the school – some taught music, others were catechists helping prepare children from the State Schools for the sacraments. The sisters visited the sick and carried out a vital support apostolate to the work of the priests.

A Catholic knew what it meant to be a Catholic. A Catholic understood their place in the Church and in society. Catholics were often known among their friends and acquaintances as Catholics. There were definable practices and traditions that Catholics adhered to – they did not eat meat on Fridays; they were marked on Ash Wednesday; they did not attend other churches for weddings or funerals. In Australia some residual sectarianism meant that Catholics were sometimes denied certain rights. This helped confirm their sense of identity.

All of this was to quite dramatically change in the years after the Second Vatican Council.

Baby Boomer generation

This is the Church that the Baby Boomers inherited. However it was this generation that was being stirred by the profound social movements which were reshaping Western culture. Whether it was student activism, or experimenting with drugs, or being enticed by wanting greater sexual freedom, or simply imbibing the optimism of peace and love, this generation was caught up in a whirlwind of new attitudes and ideas. Combined with this heady mixture there was a new spirit sweeping the Church as a result of the teachings of the Second Vatican Council which some saw as the Church coming to terms with modernity. This generation was involved with experimentation in the Liturgy, a focus on the rights of individual conscience and challenges to many traditional Catholic practices.

Those who grew up in the period after Vatican II were influenced by the attitudes that emphasised the newness of the Church's self identity and its openness to the world around them. They were no longer willing to accept the teachings of the Church as divinely inspired and immutable. They also took the view that they could be active protagonists of the future Church.

This was the generation who asked whether it was a sin to miss Sunday Mass. It was the generation who sought what they believed were the Gospel imperatives of love, peace and freedom, and resisted the formal authority of the Church. Many, under the banner of "the spirit" of Vatican II, believed that the Church was irrevocably changing and embracing the modern world. They believed that the Church was abandoning old ways and seeing things in a new light.

Later reflection on this period has given rise to the notion of the hermeneutic of continuity/discontinuity.[26] The Baby Boomer generation was caught up with the idea that there was a new era coming upon the Church and that the Church needed to adapt to the times. The new spirit washing over Western societies in particular proposed a breaking of the limiting shackles of the past – Victorian morality, legalism and obedience to authority.

These changes which have spanned the last 50 years can described as the "experiential shift" whereby the ultimate authority for people's lives shifted from a reliance on religious and political authority to an orientation around an individual's experiences, senses and feelings. In other words personal experience replaced reason and tradition as the basis of the authority in their lives.

This generation came to view the pursuit of self-transformation

---

26 Pope Benedict XVI's Christmas message to the Roman Curia of 22 December 2005, addressed the question of the Second Vatican Council's "hermeneutic of continuity" versus that of rupture. In this talk he said:

> On the one hand, there is an interpretation that I would call "a hermeneutic of discontinuity and rupture"; it has frequently availed itself of the sympathies of the mass media, and also one trend of modern theology. On the other, there is the "hermeneutic of reform", of renewal in the continuity of the one subject – Church which the Lord has given to us. She is a subject which increases in time and develops, yet always remaining the same, the one subject of the journeying People of God. The hermeneutic of discontinuity risks ending in a split between the pre-conciliar Church and the post-conciliar Church. It asserts that the texts of the Council as such do not yet express the true spirit of the Council. It claims that they are the result of compromises in which, to reach unanimity, it was found necessary to keep and reconfirm many old things that are now pointless. However, the true spirit of the Council is not to be found in these compromises but instead in the impulses toward the new that are contained in the texts.

and self-determination as the focus for life. There was a significant shift from a reliance on authority to a suspicion of institutional authority. The view developed that a person can base their positions on matters grounded in their own experience and, as they become aware of their own independence of thought, they uphold the right for tolerance and acceptance of the views of others. Tolerance was promoted as the key virtue.

One particularly revolutionary aspect of Vatican II was the priority given to individual conscience in relation to freedom of religion. In *Dignitatis Humanae*, the "Declaration on Religious Liberty", the Council recognised that "contemporary man is becoming increasingly conscious of the dignity of the human person; more and more people are demanding that men should exercise fully their own judgement and a responsible freedom in their actions and should not be subject to the pressure of coercion but be inspired by a sense of duty".[27] Furthermore, "he is bound to follow this conscience faithfully in all his activity so that he may come to God, who is his last end. Therefore he must not be forced to act contrary to his conscience. Nor must he be prevented from acting according to his conscience, especially in religious matters".[28]

Generally there was a significant eroding of the sense of Catholic identity. Many wanted to be able to fit more comfortably within the social environment of the day. Dialogue was favoured in the place of confrontation. Ecumenism was to replace proselytism. Respectful tolerance was favoured to the delineation of differences. Generally there was a desire for a synthesis between the Church and society. However the risk was that this synthesis would become assimilation. Catholics would become citizens of this world first and the distinctive

---
27 *Dignitatis Humanae*, n. 1.
28 Ibid., n. 3.

nature of being Catholic would be lost. In many ways this is what happened.

This generation felt it had the right to question the Church on its teaching and practices. This generation believed in personal choice and believed in the right to freedom of opinion. It was this generation that would then raise up Generation X.

Generation X

Richard Rymarz in an excellent study has mapped the changes in attitude towards the Catholic faith in Generations X and Y.[29] He has drawn extensively on sociological and psychological studies which identify the general characteristics of these generations.

Generation X was to reap the whirlwind sweeping the Church. For them nothing was fixed or solid. Experimentation was widespread as many in the Church sought to map a way forward. They were a generation who became disengaged with the Church which was unable to offer clarity and direction. They were a lost generation.

The clearest indicator of this was the abandonment of regular practice of attending Sunday Mass. Robert Dixon from the Australian Bishops' Office for Pastoral Research put Mass attendance for Gen X at 8 per cent based on 2006 count of Mass attendees in Australia. This marks an extraordinary decline in practice.

Baptised Gen Xers would identify as Catholic but would be more at home with the notion that what was important to them was a certain spiritual sense to life rather than acceptance of the Catholic faith. The catch phrase that captured this was "I am spiritual not religious". Such an approach which was more amenable to this generation enables a person to maintain some general sense of allegiance to the Church

---

29 *The New Evangelisation, Issues and Challenges for Catholic Schools*, Modotti Press, 2012.

but not sense any need to conform to the demands of being Catholic – like attending Sunday Mass. It is Catholicism on their own terms.

Another significant shift in perspective for this generation was the focus on moral values rather than on dogmatic beliefs. Gen X saw in social justice an expression of their Catholic faith. Many schools seeking to engage with their students took up social justice as the focus of their religious programmes. This generation saw no value in beliefs, but wanted to engage in social action. Later the cause of the environment became the particular focus of social concern.

The pedagogy employed at this time in religious education was experiential rather than doctrinal. Students were encouraged to explore their own world and were not exposed to the great traditions of Catholic thought. An ignorance of Catholic tradition grew in them and their sense of identity as a Catholic lapsed.

This generation had a low religious socialisation. Their parents, the Baby Boomers, had lost much incisive Catholic identity and so were not able to pass on Catholic culture in any decisive way. This generation had little knowledge of Catholic teachings, traditions and practices. In an era that began to speak of "Catholic ethos" young people had little to hold on to as what in fact defined their Catholic identity. They lacked any real sense of being Catholic.

Religious socialisation is assisted by discernible markers, for example, "our family is a Catholic family because we say the Rosary together". Many of the markers disappeared from Catholic life. Family life in many Catholic families was much the same as that of the people next door who were not Catholic. There were few expressions of distinctive practices and customs, except for key moments like Christmas and Easter, and Lent. Generation X Catholics were content with who they were. There was not a sense of guilt at being less than involved with the Church.

Generation Y

For the following generation, Gen Y, these trends would increase. They would grow up with ever weakening formative experiences to nurture their Catholic identity. In tests which list various indicators of Catholic identification the comparison between Gen X and Gen Y confirm an increased disaffiliation.[30]

Indicators like belief in God, belief in life after death, attending Mass and being willing to pray revealed that this generation was slipping either further from an understanding of what it means to be Catholic. Self-identification as a Catholic declined significantly. Baptised Catholics from Gen Y began to identify as much with ideas from the New Age, or with secular moral attitudes, and even with the views of the New Atheists as with Catholic beliefs. Conviction about belief in God or life after death was reduced as Gen Y becomes tentative or agnostic on these issues.

What is in evidence is not so much the explicit rejection of the Catholic faith as rather a general vagueness and uncertainty. This led many to begin searching for meaning and direction. Research in the United States has proposed the concept of "Moralistic Therapeutic Deism" as a descriptor of the spiritual situation of Gen Y.[31] This term depicts the fact that such spiritual orientation is not transformative, but rather a comfort in the midst of uncertainty. This generation has shown a low capacity for moral reasoning and will slide into individual preference on moral matters.

---

30 See Rymarz, p. 76.
31 Proposed by Christian Smith and Melinda Lindquist Denton, *Soul Searching: The Religious and Spiritual Lives of American Teenagers* (New York, Oxford University Press, 2005). Quoted by Rymarz, p. 62.

Changes to marriage and family

The family is the foundational environment for the transmission of the faith from one generation to the next. The family has been called the "domestic Church".[32] The family is also the foundation to society. When social change affects marriage and family life it has profound effects not only on the faith of all concerned but also on the quality of life within the society.

Over the past 50 years there have been very significant changes to the way marriage and family life are approached. These changes must also be understood in order to appreciate the lived reality of many people's lives today. When we come to consider evangelisation the more we understand the circumstances of people's lives the more we are able to tailor the message to assist people to embrace the Catholic faith. The Church has much to offer in regard to marriage and family, but in order for people to embrace this rich source of understanding about marriage and family they must first draw near to the fount of truth – Jesus Christ.

An abundance of evidence from social science research confirms that healthy, stable and happy marriages are the optimal environments for the psychological, emotional and physical wellbeing of both the adults and children. However we are witnessing many social, cultural and economic changes that are having an adverse impact on marriage and family. When marriage and family are weakened both the Church and society suffer.

There are many indicators that reveal what could be termed a

---

[32] The *Catechism of the Catholic Church* (1655-1657) speaks of families being "domestic churches" where the parents are the first heralds of the faith. The home is the first school of Christian life.

"retreat from marriage" in our society.[33] It is evident that marriage is not as prized and protected as it has been in the past. For example, the age when people are getting married has risen significantly; from 30 years ago being in the early 20s to the present day when the average age is around 30. Leaving marriage to an older age creates other issues about the ability to have children. Another significant trend is that over the past 30 years the percentage of couples who are cohabiting prior to marriage has risen from 20 per cent to 60-80 per cent. Far more people remain unmarried in our society than ever before. Twice the number of children are born out of wedlock than thirty years ago. And, as is well known, the breakdown of marriages has risen considerably.

The human cost in all of this is great indeed. Children are the particular victims of marital dysfunction. They are the voiceless losers. They themselves do not experience what a stable loving marital union is and often repeat the failures of their parents. Women whose marriages break down or who have children out of wedlock are often affected economically and cannot escape low income lifestyles. A non-marital culture creates lower earning capacity and increased welfare dependency. Marital breakdown has profound consequences on the health of a society, both in terms of the quality of life and the advancement of the economy.

From 1974 to 2006 sole parents in Australia increased from 9.2 per cent to 22 per cent of families with children under 15 years of age. Two-thirds of these families need Social Security benefits in order to survive and the cost to the government has escalated from $160 million in 1973-74 to $2.9 billion currently.

---

33 I am indebted to the extensive compilation of research on changes of attitudes to marriage and family explored in Kevin Andrews' book, *Maybe I Do, Modern Marriage and the Pursuit of Happiness*. Connor Court, 2012.

The introduction of no-fault divorce has meant that couples can dissolve their union relatively easily. There was a prevailing view behind the legislation that it is better for couples in an unhappy union to separate. However, children involved suffer greatly from the actions of their parents. There are many family studies which now question the wisdom of no-fault divorce.[34] Governments and churches realise that there is a need to rekindle an appreciation of the importance of a pro-marriage culture. It is important to assist couples to assume greater responsibility to work out their differences for the sake of the children.

A stable marriage has a marked positive effect on health and welfare of the couple. Married people tend to live longer than single people; issues like alcoholism and mental disease are less prevalent among married people. Relationship breakdown, on the other hand, is a major cause of depression and suicide.

For children a stable happy marriage is the best source for emotional stability and good physical and mental health. The experience of divorce has both short-term and long-term effects and heightens the risk of poor physical and mental health.

The cultural changes which we are witnessing can be identified as being stimulated by the use of contraception which encourages relationships separated from their life-giving dimension. Cohabitation has fostered confusion about the interrelatedness of intimacy and commitment. Prolonged autonomy as an individual earner has fostered a reluctance to accept the restrictions that marriage and family naturally entail. The increased educational opportunities available to women have led them to want to pursue a career and they are often torn in establishing an appropriate work/life balance.

---

34 See Kevin Andrews, *Maybe I Do*, pp 155-6, 251-2.

In general we can say that there is a rise in individualism in society, a loosening of marriage bonds and evolving gender relationships. This has meant that people are marrying less, choosing to cohabit before marriage, more likely to divorce and have fewer children. One result of all this is that the population is ageing and many Western nations do not have replacement birth-rates.[35]

One of the reasons for an increase in cohabitation is a change in the understanding of the nature of marriage. One term used more frequently these days is that of "soul mate". We hear couples on their wedding day that they are "marrying my best friend". The focus of the relationship in such an understanding is on the couple themselves. The desire is for a relationship that is personally fulfilling. This is all very good. However, the notion of self-giving commitment and of the generation of children as integral to the meaning of marriage is not necessarily encompassed in such terms.

It has generally been understood that cohabiting helps a couple see if they are suited. However there is abundant evidence that couples slide into cohabitation and often as they become more mutually dependent they slide into marriage. Cohabitation works against a careful and well prepared decision.

Attitudes towards marriage have changed significantly in recent decades. With a weakening of a marriage culture individuals are open to damaging experiences which then lessen their ability to find happiness in life and create environments conducive to the healthy nurturing of children. This, in turn, has serious consequences for the transmission of faith. It means that the Church has to deal with

---

35 For the population of a country to remain stable women must have an average of 2.1 children. At the present time Japan has 1.4, Italy has 1.2, Spain has 1.15. Russia's population has declined every year since 1992 and on present trends is likely to fall from 143 million to 107 million in 2050.

many people who have been damaged by their marriage and family experiences. Evangelisation may need to involve processes to assist people in coming to terms with their hurts and pains of the past.

Global culture

The global culture which impacts on us constantly by means of the media is constantly changing. Today a teenager in Delhi or Rio de Janeiro or in New York is likely to listen to the same music, see the same popular "blockbuster" movies and play the same computer games. They communicate via Facebook and Twitter and have the mobile phone as the principal agent for their personal communication. This culture is not a static but a dynamic reality. Ideas, images and values are being fed into their minds. To evangelise we need to understand what is happening in the global culture and be alert to the effects of the various media. In particular we need to understand the contemporary mind.

Today culture is not restricted to a particular national ethos, let alone to the influence of the Church or the family. It is being created in the global mass media – films, songs, computer games, advertising, new technology products. People are living increasingly within the virtual world. While there is no conspiracy to develop a particular culture or seek to shape people's attitudes (media is driven by market forces and not ideology) yet there is no doubt that there are definable elements present in most media and these are being transmitted to the contemporary generation of young people in particular.

We can identify three world views that are prevalent today. They are secularism, individualism and relativism.

Secularism means that a person lives for this world alone. Its focus is on enjoying life, getting the most out of life. The pursuit of good experiences found in entertainment or travel is a high priority. Such an attitude focuses on all that life offers as though there is nothing else.

Individualism means focusing on the self. This attitude fosters what much of the advertising industry seeks to promote: that the most important person in the world is me. People make decisions on the basis of what is best for their own interests. It is expressed in the view that people instinctively query, "what's in it for me?"

Relativism means that a person does not believe in objective truth and sets out to find their own truth, simply "what works for me". Such people take the attitude that "You can have your truth and I will have my truth." Such people will live according to what they believe to be right.

It is not as though such people oppose God, but simply they have come to a place where they believe that God is not needed. God is largely irrelevant to their lives. They find that they can live as though God does not exist. Or if He does exist, then they expect that God has no particular problems with the way they are living. They think that they are basically good and reasonable human beings.

Living as though God does not exist

In 1988, Pope John Paul with clear insight summarised what he saw happening in the First World cultures:

> Whole countries and nations where religion and the Christian life were formerly flourishing and capable of fostering a viable and working community of faith, are now put to a hard test, and in some cases, are even undergoing a radical transformation, as a result of a constant spreading of an indifference to religion, of secularism and atheism. This particularly concerns countries and nations of the so-called

First World, in which economic well-being and consumerism, even if coexistent with a tragic situation of poverty and misery, inspires and sustains a life lived "as if God did not exist". This indifference to religion and the practice of religion devoid of true meaning in the face of life's very serious problems, are no less worrying and upsetting when compared with declared atheism.[36]

In countries which have been traditionally Christian the Pope noted the rise of a culture where people live "as though God does not exist". This approach to life is quite prevalent in many Western countries and through the influence of media is spreading universally.

The post-Christian agnostic

We could describe those who have had some Christian background through family and perhaps schooling but who have now abandoned Christian faith as post-Christian agnostics. They are agnostic to the extent that they have not so much rejected Christianity formally and embraced atheism – though some have – but rather they have withdrawn from a position of faith and are uncertain about spiritual things. They may believe in the existence of some other power but they have no clarity about the nature of something beyond this life.

There are some defining characteristics of the post-Christian agnostic. As post-Christians they have had some exposure to Christianity both within their personal backgrounds and they have been exposed to the culture of Christianity to some extent. They have come to a position that Christianity and the Church hold nothing for them. They are people who would describe themselves as "spiritual but not religious". They do not see themselves as holding to any religious system.

---

36 *Christifideles Laici*, n. 34.

As agnostics they are uncertain about the nature of God. They will often say that they believe that there must be some form of higher power but they cannot define the nature of god and do not imagine god as being capable of intervening in their lives. Generally, however, they do not investigate this question and leave it as an unknown in their life.

Because there is a sense of a higher being, they are often open to receiving particular beliefs from a variety of sources. For instance, they may have a vague acceptance of reincarnation, or see the value in using a particular mantra or believe that yoga helps them spiritually. They may be attracted to the idea of guardian angels or seek direction for their lives from tarot cards. In other words, while rejecting religion they do embrace various ideas or practices that have spiritual roots.

One aspect to the mindset of the post-Christian agnostic that is important for the new evangelisation is that such people are very sceptical about religious authority, about organised religion and particularly about the Church. Often they carry strong prejudices about the Church which they see as out of touch, judgmental, and excessively demanding. While they may be attracted so some aspects of Christianity, like meditation, they would not envisage themselves ever attending a formal Church activity.

The post-Christian agnostic has a scientific mindset. They require matters of spiritual belief to be proved. They struggle with the notion of faith. The issue is that they approach Christianity and transcendental realities as a whole from an intellectual perspective. Things must be processed by the mind and what does not satisfy the mind is not accepted. The new evangelisation while it does contain an intellectual element must address the human heart.

To evangelise the post-Christian agnostic it is necessary to help them move to another plane of approach to Christianity. It can be beneficial not to focus on the essential Christian message from the outset as this will just lead to the person bunkering down in their quasi scientific approach to things. One avenue of approach is to talk about the nature of the human person. This is an arena where personal experience can be shared and the basis for a common ground in discussion found. In such a discussion the experience of love, trust, hope and so on can be raised. These experiences cannot be scientifically proven or analysed. They are common human experiences. In other words we have begun to consider other sources of knowledge and experience. It opens up the question of the nature of relationships in human life. From this place the conversation can move to discussion of God as One who desires to have a personal relationship with us.

Pope Benedict XVI understood this situation well and his teaching constantly addressed the question of faith and how faith can lead to the flourishing of the human person. This is a valuable pointer as to the thrust of the new evangelisation.

Religious affiliation in Australia

In Australia the 2011 census revealed some sobering information. The Catholic Church is the largest single religious group in Australia – one in four Australians is Catholic. The next biggest group, coming in at 22 per cent, are those who claim to have no religion.

This trend is not limited to Australia but is reflected across the Western world. More and more people are claiming to have no religion at all. This is a new phenomenon in world history. In the past people always believed in something. Now we face a new phenomenon and the Church is challenged to meet this new situation. In one sense it is more difficult because people have the attitude that they know about Christianity and have dismissed it as not having any relevance to their lives.

Claims of the Secularists

Those who are advocates of secularising Australian society take much heart from statistics like these and are becoming more strident in expressing their views, and wanting Australian society to be free of religious cultural elements. We hear the claims that society, indeed the world, is moving beyond religion. In particular Christianity is singled out as being in a state of decline.

Certainly the rise in those who "live as though God does not exist" presents a new phenomenon in human history. Cultures have always had at their heart religious beliefs and practices of one kind or another. The great cultures have had very sophisticated spiritual and moral systems built upon a belief in a supreme being. Secularism presents a new phenomenon.

Secularists are emboldened now to seek to eliminate the presence of Christian influence in various spheres of life. Religious freedom is under threat. For example, the *Abortion Law Reform Act* in Victoria[37] denied the right of doctors and nurses to refuse to be involved in or refer abortions on grounds of conscience. A person is in effect forced under law to act in a way contrary to their conscience. This is a serious breach in what we would regard as sacrosanct in our society: freedom of conscience and religious belief. This sets a very significant precedent. Other religious freedoms could be threatened

---

37 The Act was passed in the Victorian Parliament in 2008. The particular issue that is of concern is found in section 8 of the Act whereby a medical practitioner is required to actively facilitate an abortion. A woman demanding an abortion can require a doctor to comply with her wishes.

in the time ahead. In Britain the Church has had to close its adoption agencies because they are required by law to allow adoption by same sex couples. This goes against our Catholic beliefs, but there is no exception given to Church agencies.

In the past we have struggled on matters concerning the sacredness of human life; now we are facing challenges on questions of the nature of marriage and family; we are beginning to experience threats to freedom of conscience and freedom of religion. Under the cover of terms like anti-discrimination and women's health, a process of social engineering is taking place. Secularists have set out to replace the Christian ethical underpinning of society with their own ideology based on accepted public opinion on issues. Public opinion is won over by carefully crafted campaigns, and Christians often find themselves on the back foot.

Eclipse of God/Eclipse of Man

One of the arguments that is put forward strongly against Christians, and Catholics in particular, is that Christians should keep their faith to themselves. There is a concerted effort to convince believers that faith is a personal matter and should be left in the private sphere. The public sphere they argue should not be subjected to religious thinking and morality coming from a religious perspective.

There is a fallacy in this line of thinking that needs to be exposed. Very simply what is at stake here is the future wellbeing of society. For believers to abandon the public sphere to secularist approaches is to allow society to become subject to forces that lack an essential fidelity to the true nature of man.

Pope John Paul captured the issue in a simple and compelling phrase – the eclipse of God will lead to the eclipse of man. He developed this argument in his great encyclical on Life – *Evangelium Vitae*. In describing the struggle between the "culture of life" and the "culture of death" he adds:

> ... when the sense of God is lost, there is also a tendency to lose the sense of man, of his dignity and his life; in turn, the systematic violation of the moral law, especially in the serious matter of respect for human life and its dignity, produces a kind of progressive darkening of the capacity to discern God's living and saving presence.[38]

His critique of the tendencies in modern society is clear and strong:

> The eclipse of the sense of God and of man inevitably leads to a practical materialism, which breeds individualism, utilitarianism and hedonism. Here too we see the permanent validity of the words of the Apostle: "And since they did not see fit to acknowledge God, God gave them up to a base mind and to improper conduct" (Romans 1:28). The values of being are replaced by those of having. The only goal which counts is the pursuit of one's own material well-being. The so-called "quality of life" is interpreted primarily or exclusively as economic efficiency, inordinate consumerism, physical beauty and pleasure, to the neglect of the more profound dimensions – interpersonal, spiritual and religious – of existence.[39]

Once God is removed from the schema of human life and from the schema of society then it inevitably will lead to an unraveling of human life and of human society: the eclipse of God will lead to the eclipse of man.

---

38 *Evangelium Vitae*, n. 21.
39 Ibid., n. 23.

Thus for the sake of the future of our society we cannot allow ourselves to be sidelined in the public debate. Nor can we allow increasing numbers of people live "as though God did not exist". We have a fundamental truth about the human person and about the nature of human life that needs to be out there in the market place. Each believer needs to be actively contributing to the public debate.

The Church now has the challenge to effectively confront the tide of secularism. There is no doubt that secularism is a strong, well organised, articulate and effective force in modern Australian society. It is gaining more and more adherents. It is sniffing victory and will try to more actively advance its cause.

The essential need for God

In the face of rising secularism the Church will need to offer an evangelising message that draws people away from a pursuit of the things of this world to seek the things of heaven. This may seem a tall order, but there is in every human being a quest for the spiritual. A secular lifestyle is often shown to be empty and unfulfilling. In moments of questioning and searching the Church needs to be there to offer its way, which is the way of Jesus Christ.

St Augustine's statement at the start of his Confessions, "God, you have made us for yourself, and our hearts are restless till they find their rest in you" is well known. There is a deep truth in what he says and it reflects his own journey to faith. St Augustine only found "rest" when he discovered faith in Jesus Christ.

The Book of Genesis records that when God made us he made us in his "image and likeness". There is a dimension to ourselves as human beings which is linked to God. The implication of this is that we cannot find ourselves as human beings apart from God.

When a person explicitly or unknowingly cuts God out of their life, they create a vacuum within themselves. They try to fill this vacuum in various ways, but it is a "God-sized" hole, and only God can fill it. Every person needs God. No person is complete without God. No human society will be healthy without God. No human life can find its ultimate meaning without God. No human being can find their final destiny without God.

We have the answer to the human quest. We have a treasure in our Catholic faith. We have the "Words of eternal Life" because we believe. This is what every person needs. This is what our society needs.

A post-script on the increasing incidence of depression

An American psychologist, Professor Martin Seligman, claimed that the rich Western countries are facing an "epidemic of depression".

Seligman identifies four causes for the rise of depression. Firstly, he speaks of the rise of individualism which he describes it as the "big I and the small we". Secondly he mentions what he calls the "depredations of the self-esteem movement". Third in his mind is the rise of victimhood where people blame others for their misfortunes. And finally he speaks of "short cuts to happiness" and refers to the pursuit of instant gratification − in junk food, television, shopping, drugs, loveless sex, spectator sport, chocolate, and so on.

His insights align with what we have been discussing as to the cultural changes in contemporary society. They are not achieving healthy results. An other-directed life is a key path to happiness. The ultimate other-directedness is towards God, the Creator and destiny of humanity. The self-esteem movement focuses on the achievement of personal success by way of positive thinking. People try to save themselves.

His mention of victimhood highlights the tendency of people today to avoid personal responsibility. To be able to say, "I have sinned", is a liberating opportunity for inner growth.

His comments on the shortcuts to happiness reflect the tendency to live for this world alone and to seek personal happiness in materialistic terms. It is not a recipe for happiness.

5

Church Teaching on Evangelisation

The mission of the Church has always been understood as the evangelising of those who have never heard of Christ. The great surges in the missionary endeavour has often been linked, particularly in the second millennia of Christianity with the discovery of peoples who have not known Christ. In 1622 at the of the missionary surge in the Americas, Africa and in Asia Pope Gregory XV established the Sacred Congregation for the Propagation of the Faith as a coordinating body for the Church's missionary endeavour. This body became a very powerful organisation. It established printing presses to produce Catholic materials in the languages of the mission territories. It fostered the education of missionaries preparing them for work in often very difficult situations. It oversaw the establishment of ecclesiastical structures in newly established churches.

Propaganda Fidei as it was known expressed the orientation of the Church towards the evangelisation of areas of the world not previously penetrated by Christianity. However, modern times have led to changed circumstances. There are no longer eras of discovery. In many countries small churches are now established. While there is not the need for vast numbers of missionaries as in past times, the task of mission remains in the Church.

Aware of the significant changes in the approach to mission during the second part of the 20th century Pope John Paul produced his eighth encyclical, *Redemptoris Missio*, in 1990. Its subtitle is significant, "On the permanent validity of the Church's missionary mandate."

This encyclical emphasised the continuing urgency for missionary work but also addressed the changed circumstances in which the Church finds itself.

To understand his teaching it will be useful to look at the key antecedent documents of the Church's magisterium.

Lumen Gentium

Paragraph 16 in *Lumen Gentium*, the document on the Church from Vatican II, has had a significant influence on the question of evangelisation. The teaching of the Council was that it is possible to be saved without explicit faith in Jesus Christ and incorporation into the Church. The text states: "Those also can attain to salvation who through no fault of their own do not know the Gospel of Christ or His Church, yet sincerely seek God and moved by grace strive by their deeds to do His will as it is known to them through the dictates of conscience."[40]

Many have taken this sentence that many will be saved without having heard the Gospel as a reason to ask: why do we need to preach the Gospel? This particular text has had a significant effect on the missionary zeal of the Church. So we need to examine this teaching a little more closely.

Not only has this statement called into question the urgency of mission but it has also raised the question concerning the existence of hell. Some claim that even if hell exists there is no-one in it. Others have taken up with an ancient concept of apocatastasis,[41] or

---

40 I am indebted to Ralph Martin's *Will Many Be Saved?* for this section. The book is a significant contribution to the correct understanding of *Lumen Gentium*, 16.

41 The word is Greek meaning restoration to the original condition. It is the name given to the theological opinion that at the end of time all creatures will share in the salvation won by Christ, both devils and human beings.

the universality of salvation. Even theologians of the stature of Karl Rahner and Hans Urs von Balthasar have argued for universalism[42]. What they argue is that because Christ has redeemed mankind and because of the gracious love of God whose power far surpasses human sin, all men and women will in fact freely and finally surrender to God in love and be saved.

This position does fly in the face of Scripture and the tradition of the Church. For example, Jesus taught, "Enter by the narrow gate; for the gate is wide and the way is easy, that leads to destruction, and those who enter by it are many. For the gate is narrow and the way is hard, that leads to life, and those who find it are few" (Matthew 7:13-14).

However the *Lumen Gentium* text does go on to list certain specific conditions in which it is possible that a person who does not know Christ can be saved. They must not be culpable for their ignorance of Christ. They must be seeking God with a sincere heart and live their lives in conformity with what they know as the good. The text states: "But often men, deceived by the Evil One, have become vain in their reasonings and have exchanged the truth of God for a lie, serving the creature rather than the Creator. Or some there are who, living and dying in this world without God, are exposed to final despair."

This statement reflects Romans 1 which speaks of the general situation of people who do not have the benefit of faith to guide and strengthen them to resist temptation and live an upright life. Any suggestion of optimism surrounding the capacity for human beings of their own ability to be saved is tempered by this statement. The reality of sin, original and personal, places heavy burdens on each

---

42 Karl Rahner's universalist theology led him to promote the concept of the "anonymous Christian" while Hans Urs von Balthasar' proposed a "hope" that all will be saved.

individual and the human history reveals the extent of human sin. What St Paul described in Romans 1 is true of humanity. Hostility to God, denial of the truth, justification of abominable behaviour mark human history.

We could summarise the teaching of this paragraph as saying that while it is possible for each person to be saved without effectively hearing the Gospel this is not probable. The Council concluded this paragraph with a reiteration of the imperative to preach the Gospel: "Wherefore to promote the glory of God and procure the salvation of all of these, and mindful of the command of the Lord, "Preach the Gospel to every creature", the Church fosters the missions with care and attention."

Ad Gentes

A useful place to start is to examine the document, *Ad Gentes*, which was Vatican II's Decree on Missionary Activity, published in 1965. The document which specifically addressed the question of the evangelising mission of the Church needs to be seen within the context of the overall thrust of the Second Vatican Council. Pope John XXIII called the Council with the intention that it would enable the Church to proclaim the Gospel more effectively to the modern world.

Later popes would present their own teaching on evangelisation against the background of the Council. Pope Paul released his milestone document, *Evangelii Nuntiandi,* on the tenth anniversary of the closing of the Council. Pope John Paul released his encyclical, *Redemptoris Missio*, on the 25th anniversary of the closing of the Council. Thus, the popes very deliberately were building on the teaching of the Second Vatican Council.

Ad Gentes was developed under the direction of Superior General of the Divine Word Missionaries, Johannes Schütte, and with the contribution of theologians of the calibre of Yves Congar, Joseph Ratzinger and Karl Rahner. A draft of the document was presented at the last session and, after a number of last minute revisions, was unanimously approved by the Council Fathers on the last day of the Council.

Ad Gentes, has made a significant contribution to the Church's teaching on mission. In paragraph 2 of the Decree the ultimate foundation for the church's missionary activity is expressed as the participation in the mission of the Son and the Holy Spirit. By virtue of baptism which draws every Christian into the very life of the Trinity the Church becomes "missionary by its very nature". What this statement emphasises is that that mission is not just something the church does, but rather it is constitutive of its very being. To be a Christian means to be missionary. The entire church is missionary by nature. This also opened up the idea that the mission of the Church was not confined to priests and religious or those with a missionary heart. It set in motion an idea that has come into greater clarity over time – every Catholic by virtue of baptism is engaged with the mission of the Church.

A second important aspect to the understanding of the notion of mission in this Decree is that the mission of the Church is not confined to "mission territories", but is to be its basic attitude wherever it is. The Church should be missionary wherever it exits. Parishes should not see themselves only as pastoral centres but should be reaching out with the Gospel message. This thought also will come to have increasing significance as the Church grappled with the decline in faith in traditionally Christian countries.

The Decree makes the point that evangelisation must be tailored to the particular cultural setting where the Church is. In paragraph 11 the Decree states: "In order that they may be able to bear more fruitful witness to Christ ... let them share in cultural and social life by the various undertakings and enterprises of human living; let them be familiar with their national and religious traditions." Once again this is an important idea. It gives attention to the reality of culture. Evangelisation must not only address the conversion of individuals but must also seek to shape culture. It must be the leaven in the dough. This means that evangelisation must consider the cultural situation and find ways to influence the culture. In this text Christians are being called to be real participants in the cultural and political life of the nations in which they live in order to be able to evangelise the particular culture.

The teaching of the Decree also acknowledged the need to plant the faith in a way that recognised the particular culture of the people. Christianity cannot just sweep the culture of the people away. It must respect the legitimate aspects of the local culture. In paragraph 22 the Decree stated: "Thus it will be more clearly seen in what ways faith may seek for understanding, with due regard for the philosophy and wisdom of these peoples; it will be seen in what ways their customs, views on life, and social order, can be reconciled with the manner of living taught by divine revelation."

The Decree on the missionary activity of the Church provided some important foundations for the development of the notion of evangelisation which was to become the key term to describe the Church's missionary mandate. While the Decree had missionaries in mission countries very much in mind, the emphasis on the universality of the missionary mandate entrusted to the Church provided an important basis for several key documents that were to follow.

Evangelii Nuntiandi

The 1975 Apostolic Exhortation of Pope Paul, *Evangelii Nuntiandi*, was written in an atmosphere where there was some doubt and uncertainty about the nature of the mission of the Church in the world. The Vatican II document on the Church, *Lumen Gentium*, had taught that women and men could be saved outside the Church and without any explicit faith in Christ.[43] There was also the situation in South America which promoted liberation theology, shifting the mission of the Church from the spiritual to the temporal realm. The recognition of the worth and value of other religions caused some to wonder about trying to penetrate these cultures with the Christian message.

It was in this context that Paul VI convoked the 1974 Synod of Bishops with the theme "Evangelisation in the Modern World". It was this document that proposed the word "evangelisation" as the best descriptor of the mission of the Church in the world today.

Like *Ad Gentes*, Pope Paul emphasised the essential missionary nature of the church. In this document it is Jesus' mission of preaching and teaching that is the essential paradigm for the mission of the Church. Thus Pope Paul said, "As an evangeliser, Christ first of all proclaims a kingdom, the kingdom of God; and this is so important that, by comparison, everything else becomes 'the rest,' which is 'given in addition.' Only the kingdom therefore is absolute and it makes everything else relative."[44]

The Pope emphasised that Jesus both *taught* about God's Kingdom in his preaching and parables and *demonstrated* its reality by his works of healing and exorcism.[45] It is on this basis the Pope can definitively

---

43 See *Lumen Gentium*, n 16. See Ralph Martin, *Will many be saved?* Ralph offers a thorough study of the text and its implications for evangelisation.
44 *Evangelii Nuntiandi*, n. 8.
45 Ibid., nn. 11-12.

state that "evangelisation is in fact the grace and vocation proper to the Church, her deepest identity. She exists in order to evangelise".[46]

It is important to note that the pope insists that the church needs to be evangelised itself before it takes on the task of evangelisation. It must constantly listen to the Word of God; it must constantly be on the road of conversion.[47]

The document insists on the strong link between Jesus' mission and the church. The Pope insists on the fact that evangelisation is an ecclesial task through and through. Evangelisation is "not accomplished without her, and still less against her".[48]

Because the Church is essentially missionary every member of the Church is called to participate in the Church's mission: "the work of each individual member is important for the whole", he says.[49] The Pope does not want to reduce missionary work to only certain people in the Church, like members of missionary congregations or the hierarchy. He highlights the universal call to all members of the Church to be involved in evangelisation.

An important point the document makes is that evangelisation is not to be limited just to individuals but must also seek to penetrate cultures, "not in a purely decorative way, as it were, by applying a thin veneer, but in a vital way, in depth and right to their very roots".[50]

There is an important section of the document devoted to the subject of evangelisation and liberation. The Pope insists that evangelisation is not to be reduced to political or economic wellbeing. The spiritual dimension of the Gospel is actually the source of humanity's

---

46 *Evangelii Nuntiandi*, n. 14.
47 Ibid., n. 15.
48 Ibid., n. 16.
49 Ibid., n. 15.
50 Ibid., n. 20.

deepest liberation. He says that violence is never to be sanctioned, because "violence always provokes violence and irresistibly engenders new forms of oppression and enslavement which are often harder to bear than those from which they claimed to bring freedom".[51] The Pope is clearly commenting on liberation theology in South America and on the participation of priests and religious in armed resistance to oppression.

When he comes to address the question of how to evangelise the Pope speaks of the need for creativity and the development of new and effective ways of communicating the Gospel message to people of this time. As Pope Paul says:

> The obvious importance of the content of evangelisation must not overshadow the importance of the ways and means. This question of "how to evangelise" is permanently relevant, because the methods of evangelising vary according to the different circumstances of time, place and culture, and because they thereby present a certain challenge to our capacity for discovery and adaptation. On us particularly, the pastors of the Church, rests the responsibility for reshaping with boldness and wisdom, but in complete fidelity to the content of evangelisation, the means that are most suitable and effective for communicating the Gospel message to the men and women of our times.[52]

The document ends with a beautiful reflection on the role that the Holy Spirit plays in evangelisation (a teaching we have already discussed). The Pope declares that the Holy Spirit is the "principal agent of evangelisation".

---

51 *Evangelii Nuntiandi*, n. 37.
52 Ibid., n. 40.

Evangelii Nuntiandi set the Church on a fresh course in responding to the missionary mandate given to the Church by the Lord. The document opened up the Church to discovering a new evangelising energy. Whereas the understanding of the past tended to see the mission of the Church as the mission *ad gentes* (to foreign peoples), *Evangelii Nuntiandi* provided the impulse to see that evangelisation is the ordinary work of the Church in every setting in which it finds itself. It confirmed and developed the thought of *Ad Gentes*.

It encouraged all members of the Church to understand that they had a mission. This mission could be carried out in the immediate environment in which they lived. It laid the foundation for a new flourishing of evangelisation spearheaded particularly by lay people. This was the new impetus that caught the attention of Pope John Paul.

Redemptoris Missio

Pope John Paul became Supreme Pontiff in October 1978. He inherited a Church still in the throes of embracing the teaching of the Second Vatican Council, but a Church which was also becoming hesitant and uncertain about various aspects of its life and mission. There were burning questions about such issues as liturgical practice, the orientation of theology and the value and importance of mission.

To mark the 25th anniversary of *Ad Gentes* and the 15th anniversary of *Evangelii Nuntiandi*, Pope John Paul wrote *Redemptoris Missio*, subtitled, on the permanent validity of the Church's missionary activity.

At a press conference given soon after the publication of the encyclical, Josef Cardinal Tomko, the Prefect of the Congregation of the Evangelisation of Peoples, explained that one of the chief reasons for the encyclical was to correct a Christology being developed by some theologians that tended to obscure Christian belief that Jesus was indeed the unique and universal saviour of humanity.

While the Pope understood that people can be saved outside of explicit faith in Christ,[53] he emphasised that all grace comes through Christ, and Christ alone:

> No-one, therefore, can enter into communion with God except through Christ, by the working of the Holy Spirit. Christ's one, universal mediation, far from being an obstacle on the journey toward God, is the way established by God himself, a fact of which Christ is fully aware. Although participated forms of mediation of different kinds and degrees are not excluded, they acquire meaning and value only from Christ's own mediation, and they cannot be understood as parallel or complementary to his.[54]

The Pope's insistence on the centrality of Christ runs through every section of the encyclical. He teaches that the Kingdom of God is not a concept, a doctrine or a programme but that rather it is a person, the person of Jesus of Nazareth.[55]

The encyclical affirms the permanent validity of the evangelising mission of the Church:

> Proclamation is the permanent priority of mission. The Church cannot elude Christ's explicit mandate, nor deprive men and women of the "Good News" about their being loved and saved by God ... All forms of missionary activity are directed to this proclamation, which reveals and gives access to the mystery hidden for ages and made known in Christ (cf. Eph 3:3-9; Col 1:25-29), the mystery which lies at

---

53 See *Redemptoris Missio*, n. 10.
54 Ibid., n. 5.
55 Ibid.

the heart of the Church's mission and life, as the hinge on which all evangelisation turns.[56]

The Pope reaffirms the urgency for the Church to engage in missionary activity *ad gentes*, that is, the direct witnessing and proclamation of Christ in situations where he is not known, or where the Church is not strong enough to proclaim the Gospel fully.[57] This is mission, the Pope says, in the proper sense of the word.

He also speaks about evangelisation within established churches and what he has been calling the "new evangelisation" in churches "where entire groups of the baptised have lost a living sense of the faith, or even no longer consider themselves members of the Church, and live a life far removed from Christ and his Gospel".[58] We will explore this notion is more detail in later chapters.

The Pope is aware of the particular challenges for the preaching of the Gospel in the rapidly growing urban areas of the world, particularly those in Asia, Africa and Latin America. He also mentions the particular needs of the world's youth, which in many countries make up half the population. He mentions the needs of large numbers of the world's migrants and the conditions of poverty which often makes migration necessary.[59]

The Pope, in fact, has a very wide sense of mission. He captures in a renewed way the teaching of *Ad Gentes* that the Church is indeed "missionary by its very nature", and the teaching of *Evangelii Nuntiandi* that evangelisation is the church's "deepest identity".

---

56 Ibid., n. 44.
57 See *Redemptoris Missio*, n. 33.
58 Ibid., n. 33.
59 See Ibid., n. 37.

The issue of dialogue and proclamation

In 1991 an important document entitled "Dialogue and Proclamation" was produced by two dicasteries in Rome. It was a joint document of the Pontifical Council for Interreligious Dialogue and the Congregation for Evangelisation of Peoples. At the time there were some who felt that the role of the Church has changed since Vatican II and now its mission was principally that of dialogue. This document sought to clarify the respective roles of dialogue and proclamation in the mission of the Church.

The document clearly taught that Church's total mission is evangelisation and this is accomplished through a variety of activities including proclamation (the communication of the Gospel message) and dialogue (witness and exploration of respective religious convictions).

It was understood that the Church's task is not exercised in a void since believers from other religions through the sincere practice of their own traditions have already responded positively to God's offer of salvation through Christ. There is a pedagogy of proclamation and the Church must respect the varying capacities of people to hear the word. Proclamation must be (amongst other qualities) dialogical and there must be progress from the "seeds of the word".[60]

Interreligious dialogue and proclamation are not "on the same level" but they are both "authentic elements"[61] of evangelisation. Jesus Christ is to be proclaimed dialogically – in the Gospel spirit of

---

60 *Dialogue and Proclamation*, n. 70. In a General Audience on 9 September 1998, Pope John Paul stated: "Taking up the Council's teaching from the first Encyclical Letter of my Pontificate, I have wished to recall the ancient doctrine formulated by the Fathers of the Church, which says that we must recognise 'the seeds of the Word' present and active in the various religions" (*Ad Gentes*, n. 11; *Lumen Gentium*, n. 17).
61 Ibid., n. 77.

dialogue with due sensitivity to the circumstances. While interreligious dialogue promotes "truth and life"[62] proclamation guides people to an explicit knowledge of what God has achieved in Christ. Dialogue must be oriented towards proclamation and Christians must be ready to give an account of "the hope that is within them"[63] when this is called for.

These distinctive definitions make clear that, while dialogue is already in itself evangelisation, evangelisation cannot be reduced to dialogue. The two are different in scope. Dialogue does not seek the conversion of others to Christianity but the convergence of both dialogue partners to a deeper shared conversion to God. By contrast, proclamation invites others to become disciples of Christ in the Christian community.

Teaching of Pope Benedict XVI

Pope Benedict continued the focus on mission and evangelisation in his teaching. In his messages on World Mission Sunday he emphasised the importance of the mission *ad gentes*. In his 2012 message he said that the teaching of the Second Vatican Council "placing the Church's missionary nature at the centre of ecclesiology" was all the more urgent because the numbers of those who did not believe in Christ had actually grown.

He added, "We therefore need to recover the same apostolic zeal as that of the early Christian communities, which, though small and defenceless, were able, through their proclamation and witness, to spread the Gospel throughout the then known world."

Pope Benedict revealed his personal conviction when he spoke of the priority of evangelising which must involve "all the activities of

---

62 Ibid., n. 80.
63 *Dialogue and Proclamation*, n. 82: See I Peter 3:15.

the particular Church, all her sectors, in short, her whole being and all her work. Later in this work we will examine in closer detail the Pope Benedict's understanding of evangelisation for he made it one of the hallmark areas of his teaching.

What emerges from these papal statements is that there is a call going out to all Catholics to see evangelisation as an essential element to Catholic life.

Again this was captured by the Pope in his 2012 Mission Sunday message:

> One of the obstacles to the impetus of evangelisation is the crisis of faith, not only in the Western world, but among humanity which, however, is hungering and thirsting for God and must be invited and brought to the bread of life and the living water.

Primary evangelisation

In our previous discussion we have noted the permanent validity of the mission of the Church *ad gentes*. This we can call "primary or first evangelisation". Over the history of the Church we have seen times of great missionary endeavour, surges in evangelical fervour. In our immediate past history we can see that there was a certain missionary springtime during the 19th century. While the Church in Europe was engaged in a struggle with modernity a new missionary impetus occurred as Catholic missionaries in their thousands reached out to the newly discovered peoples of Africa, Oceania, Asia and the Americas.

In some ways this missionary expansion provided a means to rejuvenate the life and faith of the Church. Missionaries carried a strong universal Catholic spirit. They were servants of the Church and its mission. The missionaries felt that they were sons and defenders of a Church that was being persecuted. They were kept on the defensive by the rise of liberalism in their own countries.

When we speak of primary or first evangelisation we are referring to the announcing of the Christian Gospel to peoples who have never heard it. This evangelisation remains a major task for the Church in our time. Yes, the Catholic Church is now in nearly every country on earth, yet there remains vast groups of peoples who have not been exposed to the Christian Gospel.

As we have noted Pope John Paul, in his eighth encyclical, *Redemptoris Missio*, spoke of the "permanent validity of the Church's missionary mandate". In this document he emphasised the importance of the Church's spiritual focus, and particularly rejected any views of salvation and mission that would focus on humanity's earthly needs while remaining, as he put it, "closed to the transcendent". The mission of the Church remains that of proclaiming the message of salvation which is to be found only in and through Jesus Christ.

The Pope states in *Redemptoris Missio*: "Proclamation is the permanent priority of mission. The Church cannot elude Christ's explicit mandate, nor deprive men and women of the 'Good News' about their being loved and saved by God" (n. 44). Then he quotes *Evangelii Nuntiandi*: "Evangelisation will always contain – as the foundation, centre and at the same time the summit of its dynamism – a clear proclamation that, in Jesus Christ ... salvation is offered to all people, as a gift of God's grace and mercy."

Thus he concludes, "All forms of missionary activity are directed to this proclamation, which reveals and gives access to the mystery hidden for ages and made known in Christ (cf. Eph 3:3-9; Col 1:25-29), the mystery which lies at the heart of the Church's mission and life, as the hinge on which all evangelisation turns" (n. 44).

This important document set out to re-invigorate the missionary fervour of the Church in the face of conflicting ideas about the value of primary evangelisation. He addressed questions which arose in the light of liberation theology in Latin America, of the pursuit of inter-religious dialogue, and of a certain embarrassment about the colonial record of Europe.

In the beginning of the document the Pope stated:

> In the name of the whole Church, I sense an urgent duty to repeat this cry of St Paul. From the beginning of my Pontificate I have chosen to travel to the ends of the earth in order to show this missionary concern. My direct contact with peoples who do not know Christ has convinced me even more of the urgency of missionary activity, a subject to which I am devoting the present encyclical (n. 1).

This, in the Pope's mind, remains the primary work of the Church.

Pope John Paul wrote *Redemptoris Missio* precisely because he was concerned that the missionary zeal for primary evangelisation was waning. He was concerned that the influence of liberation theology in South America was redirecting people to strive for earthly improvement without seeking to meet the spiritual needs of the people. The threat posed by liberation theology was that it sought to redefine what evangelisation is. This remains an issue in some quarters in the Church today where the social mission of the Church has become isolated from its spiritual mission.

The Pope also saw that interest in interreligious dialogue caused people to question the importance of preaching Christ. This is an important question where the Church exists in non-Christian religious environments like India, Pakistan, Indonesia, Japan. The Church has committed itself to engage in dialogue with these great religious traditions, but this must not replace the work of evangelisation. We must still seek to fulfil the Great Commission: "Go out to all the world ... baptise them in the name of the Father, and of the Son and of the Holy Spirit".

The Church must continue to be an evangelising presence in the traditionally missionary countries. More particularly, many of these countries still lack basic services in health, education and housing. The Church in these countries is poor and struggles to provide financial support for many worthy services.

We are to stand in solidarity with our brothers and sisters in these newly emerging churches. There is still so much to do. We see this vision confirmed by Pope Benedict in his World Mission Day Message for this year (2012). The Pope urges the Church to be aware that Christ still has to be "drawn into the heart of history" and "meet the aspirations of each man and woman".

Towards a new evangelisation

In his letter at the dawn of the new millennium, *Novo Millennio Ineunte*, Pope John Paul declared: "Over the years I have often repeated the summons to the new evangelisation. I do so again now, especially in order to insist that we must rekindle in ourselves the impetus of the beginnings and allow ourselves to be filled with the ardour of the apostolic preaching which followed Pentecost."[64]

Pope John Paul was conscious from the very early days of his pontificate that while the mission *ad gentes* needs to be fostered and encouraged there is a new challenge that the Church must face. The term he coined to describe the Church's response to changing times was new evangelisation.

We will now address the more specific teaching of the Church, particularly through Pope John Paul, on the new evangelisation.

---
64 *Novo Millennio Ineunte*, n. 40.

6

A New Evangelisation

We have examined the development of the teaching of the Church on the subject of evangelisation from the Second Vatican Council onwards. We have seen how there has emerged a clear call to all the Church to engage in the mission entrusted to it by the Lord. Evangelisation is not an optional aspect to being Catholic. The Popes have also sensed the great needs of our time and have a sense of urgency about the work of evangelisation.

New evangelisation

Early in his pontificate Pope John Paul paid a number of visits to South America. It was here that he saw the dangers of liberation theology and that he became increasingly aware of the need for a new evangelisation of countries where the faith had become more cultural than real. It was out of this experience that he began to speak of the need for a new evangelisation.

In 1983 he addressed the Bishops of South America and said:

> The commemoration of the half millennium of evangelisation will gain its full energy if it is a commitment, not to re-evangelise but a New Evangelisation, new in its ardour, methods and expression.[65]

---

[65] Address to CELAM, 9 March 1983, Port-au-Prince, Haiti. The reference to the "half millennium" is a reference to the celebration of 500 years since the Gospel was first proclaimed in South America with the arrival of Spanish explorers.

In 1990 so strong had his conviction grown about the need for a new evangelisation that in *Redemptoris Missio* Pope John Paul made this strong and decisive comment:

> I sense that the moment has come to commit all of the Church's energies to a new evangelisation ... No believer in Christ, no institution of the Church can avoid this supreme duty: to proclaim Christ to all peoples.

With these words the Pope announced, "The hour has come for a re-evangelisation." The response of Pope John Paul to this situation is to encourage Catholics to engage in the great task of effecting a "re-evangelisation" or a "new evangelisation" of societies and cultures that have been traditionally Christian. Pope John Paul spoke of the new evangelisation with increasing frequency in the latter years of his pontificate. He considered it of vital importance for the future of the Church.

The new evangelisation expresses the fact that the Church is not only to look to places where the Gospel has not yet been preached – this missionary task remains of vital importance as we have seen – but now must direct more serious effort to evangelisation in societies that have been traditionally Christian and are experiencing the rise of sections of the population who have no faith – who live as though God does not exist.

This task is now seen as a vital mission for the Church. Pope John Paul appealed for a new evangelisation which was to be "new in its ardour, in its methods and in its expressions". The Pope called for a new boldness in engaging in the task of proclaiming the perennial message of Christ in modern situations.

In the light of these thoughts it is not surprising to see that on 28 June 2012 – the vigil of the Feasts of St Peter and Paul – Pope

Benedict established a Pontifical Council for the Promotion of the New Evangelisation.

In launching this new Pontifical Council the Pope said:

> There are regions in the world that still wait for a first evangelisation; others that received it but need more profound work; others still in which the Gospel put down roots a long time ago, giving place to a true Christian tradition, but where in the last centuries – with complex dynamics – the process of secularisation has produced a grave crisis of the sense of the Christian faith and of belonging to the Church.

He spoke of an "eclipse of the sense of God," which, he said, "constitutes a challenge to find the appropriate means to propose again the perennial truth of the Gospel of Christ".

The call to the new evangelisation means that we cannot only think of serving the primary evangelisation but we need also to look at our own backyard. Because of the pervasiveness of forces of secularism it is true that either the Church commits itself to evangelise the culture or the culture will "evangelise" the Church.

What Pope John Paul understood was that there was a changed context in which the Church now operates. While primary evangelisation must retain its priority for the Church, there is another growing mission field to which the Church must now turn its attention. This mission field will require the Church to rethink its strategies and to redirect its efforts and personnel. This new evangelisation will mean that there are new evangelisers needed for this work.

In the general context of changes in modern societies, what had been presumed in the past can no longer be presumed. For example, in the past it was expected that a young person growing up in a family that had strong faith and was engaged in the life of the Church would embrace and live out their Catholic faith. This is no longer the case. It is not that parents have failed to pass on the faith as rather their efforts to do so have been nullified by other influences from the society that now bear in on young people so pervasively.

The Church cannot presume that people will hold to their faith. It is now necessary for the Church to constantly work at the task of nurturing and fostering a life of faith. New ways are needed to nourish the life of faith.

It is not that many people today reject Christianity outright, but rather they experience their faith draining from them. Faith no longer is of central importance. Many become more "tribally" Catholic without deep convictions concerning the faith. They are often ambivalent about many of the teachings of the Church.

This is a new reality which demands that the Church develop need means to evangelise those who have some nominal association with the faith. It does mean that the Church needs to understand that evangelisation must now be the continual mode in which it operates. Evangelisation must become the constant in the Church's mission.

Characteristics of the new evangelisation

Pope John Paul spoke of this new evangelisation, though without giving a detailed description of its characteristics. In fact, though he spoke of it more and more frequently nowhere does he attempt to provide a theological description. However, as we follow his references we can discern certain key characteristics.

i *Centred on Jesus Christ*

For Pope John Paul the new evangelisation must focus on the proclamation of the person of Jesus Christ. At his first Mass as Pope in October 1987 he concluded his homily with the words "Open the

Doors to Christ". This phrase captures the tone of his pontificate and lies at the heart of what the new evangelisation is about. These are his words: "Do not be afraid! Do not be afraid to welcome Christ and to accept His power over you! Open, open wide the doors for Christ! He alone has the words of eternal life."

It is worth noting Pope Benedict at the first homily of his pontificate in April 2005 concluded using the same words, "Open the doors to Christ." These are his words:

> If we let Christ into our lives, we lose nothing, nothing, absolutely nothing of what makes life free, beautiful and great. No! Only in this friendship are the doors of life opened wide ... Yes, open, open wide the doors to Christ and you will find true life.

The decision of the Pope to echo the words of his predecessor indicated that he wished to continue in the same missionary spirit. The message that the Church presents to the world is simply this: to open your heart to Jesus Christ.

This phrase is inspired by a text of Scripture. In the Book of Revelations, chapter 3, St John receives these prophetic words from the Lord, "Behold I stand at the door and knock." The image is a striking one: the Lord stands at the door of our hearts and knocks. The Lord wants to enter our lives. It is a beautiful thought and a moving image. What is striking about this image is the humility of the Lord. It is he who stands and waits. He humbly and lovingly offers to come into our lives and share himself with us. He wants to be deeply part of our life. He knocks. He waits. It is up to us. The Pope urges the world to respond to this invitation.

The key distinguishing feature of the new evangelisation is its focus not only upon the person of Jesus Christ but his desire to enter our lives. The new evangelisation proclaims Christ and calls upon people to respond to him by opening up their hearts and lives to him.

In one way or another this should be seen as the goal for all evangelisation. We will explore this in greater detail in the next chapter.

ii *Deeply Catholic*

New evangelisation is profoundly Catholic in its presentation. There is a distinctively Catholic form of evangelisation which has notable differences from other evangelical approaches. For example, there is no aggressive "hard sell", Catholic evangelisation proposes, not imposes, as John Paul II taught.[66] Catholic evangelisation respects human freedom. It does not seek to coerce. Nor does it seek to convince by hard argument. While there is a very valuable role to be played by apologetics, in the end it is the human heart that must be moved. The exposure to Catholic truth can lead to an enlightenment of the mind, but it must move from the mind to the heart.

Catholic evangelisation is imbued with a spirit of love and freedom.[67] Pope Benedict's first encyclical, *Deus Caritas Est* (God is love) highlights the centrality of love in Christianity. Pope Benedict teaches that charity – love – is the responsibility of the Church.[68] Evangelisation is to be animated by love. The Church evangelises because it loves. In the end the Church sees evangelisation as a service of love.

Catholic evangelisation naturally offers a distinctive sacramental dimension to the Christian life. The way people are invited to respond to the evangelising message is through participation in the sacramental

---

66 Pope John Paul II, *Redemptoris Missio:* On the permanent validity of the Church's missionary mandate, n. 39.
67 Cf. Vatican II, *Ad Gentes*, nn. 2-5,12; Pope Paul VI, *Evangelii nuntiandi*, n. 26.
68 See *Deus Caritas Est*, n. 20.

life of the Church. We note that when St Peter was asked at the end of his preaching on Pentecost day "What must we do", he responded without hesitation, "You must be baptised" (Acts 2:38). The path to living the Christian life is that of participation in the sacramental life of the Church, culminating in celebrating the Holy Eucharist. The pattern of the Rite of Christian Initiation of Adults (RCIA) presents the paradigm of the process of coming into full participation in the life of the Church via its sacramental dispensation.

Catholic evangelisation will also engage with the rich tradition of prayer and spirituality which is the Church's great patrimony. Many popular devotions can be valuable aids in evangelisation as they have often grown in the Church to meet the spiritual needs of the faithful. Popular devotions offer experiential expression to dogmatic truths. It is certainly true that many Catholics have come to a new and revitalised faith by discovering the spiritual power of devotions. One current example is the Divine Mercy Devotions. The revelations to St Faustina of the mercy of God have stirred many. The simple phrase found on the image – "Jesus I trust in you" – has drawn many to a deeper trusting union with Christ.

Another tool in evangelisation is the use of classic Catholic images of Christ or the Blessed Virgin. The image of the Sacred Heart can be a powerful attractive presentation of the love of God for humanity. These images and the use of icons clearly define that the evangelical proclamation is Catholic. Sometimes this is a surprising discovery for listeners who don't necessarily identify evangelisation with the Catholic Church. Another useful tool in evangelisation is to give people a Miraculous Medal, or a set of Rosary beads, or a holy picture. In an increasingly secular environment these holy things are a tangible link with the transcendent.

The current rediscovery of Adoration of the Blessed Sacrament among Catholics, particularly the young, offers another valuable resource for evangelisation. Catholic faith in the Real Presence of Christ in the Eucharist draws them to quiet contemplation of his presence in the Blessed Sacrament. People with little sense of the sacred can be attracted by the sense of reverence and silence surrounding Catholic adoration. Explaining the mystery of the Eucharist can attract people to prayer, reflection and the search for God.

iii *Engaging people within the context of their lives*

A missionary going to a foreign country must learn the local language and adjust to the local culture. In the case of the new evangelisation it is normally within one's own culture that it is undertaken. This offers certain immediate advantages: the evangeliser is familiar with the life, customs and mindset of those to whom he or she is speaking. However, it is important for the evangeliser to attune him/herself to the actual experiences of those who may not be close to Christianity and the Church. Their life experience and the cultural milieu may be somewhat different from that of the evangeliser.

The new evangelisation engages with people within the context of their lives. What this may mean is that the evangeliser cannot operate within the "comfort" of the church community. A distinguishing feature of the new evangelisation in comparison with traditional missions and programmes of spiritual renewal is that it may take place outside of the Christian community, for example, within the everyday work situation. Those groups already active in the new evangelisation have often developed means of evangelising that are on the streets or in public situations.

Evangelisation must always meet people "where they are at", but the new evangelisation may need to specifically focus on this because many of those whom they wish to reach may have negative attitudes towards organised religion or may think that traditional Christianity has nothing to offer them. We have spoken previously about the post Christian agnostic. In order to reach them we need to be on neutral ground. They will not come to a church or be associated with anything that appears to represent organised religion. Nevertheless, it is possible to engage with them and present the Christian message.

We will investigate this in greater depth later when we discuss the "how" of the new evangelisation. At this point we can relate this need to be amongst the people to the ministry of Jesus himself. While he did preach in synagogues and in the temple in Jerusalem much of his ministry was "in the marketplace". This gives impetus to the evangelist to do things in a similar way.

Thus, in specific evangelisation activities the evangelist will move out into the community often using innovative ways to engage with people. Some examples of forms of this engagement with people are: door-to-door visitation, a coffee tent on the street outside the church, singing in public places, engaging people in conversation in the street, having debates in public locations, handing out medals or holy cards. These activities are eventually intended to draw people to meet Christ in the Catholic Church.

iv *A collaborative act of laity and priests*

The new evangelisation is a particular fruit of the emergence of ecclesial movements in the Church in recent times. Pope John Paul often acknowledged that they were spearheading this new evangelisation.[69] The Church both encourages and supports the evangelising efforts of these new movements, and at the same time can learn from them.

One of the distinguishing features of the new evangelisation

---

69 Pope John Paul II, Address to the Pontifical Council for the Laity, 1 March 1999; Cf. Meeting with Ecclesial Movements (30 May 1998).

developed by the various movements is that it is largely driven by committed lay people. The new evangelisation speaks to the laity in a special way because they are "in the world", and have many opportunities to engage with people through their contacts in everyday life. The role of lay people is also important because they are able to model what it means to be a Christian – in their individual lives, in their families and in the engagement with society in general. They, in a sense, are best suited to be the new evangelisers.

Priests and religious, though, should work alongside the lay people, each responding in their own way to the call to evangelise. Priests bring a vital ecclesial dimension to evangelisation and their service through the Sacraments – particularly Baptism and Reconciliation – is vital to the evangelising process. The new evangelisation promotes a new level of collaboration between priest and lay person. Each needs the distinctive contribution of the other. The new evangelisation is a particularly ecclesial act.

Holiness of life

There are other elements to the new evangelisation that are important to mention. The theme of holiness of life was one that was very common to the teaching of Pope John Paul. He proposed holiness of life as the standard goal for Christians. In his letter welcoming the new millennium, *Novo Millennio Ineunte*, he said, first quoting from the Second Vatican Council, "It is a duty which concerns not only certain Christians: 'All the Christian faithful, of whatever state or rank, are called to the fullness of the Christian life and to the perfection of charity'."

Catholics are called to be more than good, they are called to be holy. This is an important raising of the bar. It was one of the distinctive teachings of the Council and it became an important theme of the teaching of Pope John Paul.

The call to holiness of life invites Catholics to examine their conscience. The questions that can be asked are: Do I seek holiness? Do I seek to develop an interior spiritual life? Do I set aside time for prayer each day? Do I take time to reflect on the Word of God in Scripture and so model my behaviour on the teaching of Scripture? Do I go to Reconciliation regularly? Do I live daily with a consciousness of the presence of God?

One of the often heard criticisms of the Church is that it does not offer a deeper spirituality. Many believe that Buddhism, or Indian Gurus, or New Age concepts offer ways to get in touch with the transcendent. There is a belief that Catholicism has little to offer. This, of course, is so far from the truth. The Church has a rich spiritual tradition revealed in its saints and in a treasury of spiritual classics. Yet unless people can see in Catholics some manner of deeper spiritual life they will doubt that the Church has anything to offer.

The new evangelisation challenges all Catholics to deepen the quality of their spiritual lives and to more seriously pursue holiness of life.

Christian witness

Another element of importance for the new evangelisation is that of Christian witness. There has been a tendency in recent times for Catholics to prefer to keep their faith to themselves. It has been easier to do things this way. Certainly the prevailing attitude in the society is that one should give one's religion to oneself and not, as people say, "impose it on others".

There is a strong temptation not to speak up and express our views when subjects are raised in casual conversation. It is easier to be silent than to be seen as the odd one out. The Lord called upon his disciples to let their light shine. Without any flickers of light the darkness prevails.

Pope John Paul, in addressing missionaries in words that can be applied to all Catholics, taught:

> The first form of witness is *the very life of the missionary, of the Christian family*, and *of the ecclesial community*, which reveal a new way of living. The missionary who, despite all his or her human limitations and defects, lives a simple life, taking Christ as the model, is a sign of God and of transcendent realities. But everyone in the Church, striving to imitate the Divine Master, can and must bear this kind of witness.

The World Youth Day held in Sydney in 2008 evidenced how powerful Christian joy is to a society which seeks happiness and can only often find it by artificially manufacturing it by alcohol or drugs, or thumping music. What St Paul calls the "fruits of the Spirit" are a powerful tool of witness: love, joy, peace, patience, goodness, faithfulness, gentleness, self-control (Gal 5:22). The young people who were full of faith gave striking witness to the fruits of a life of faith.

Catholics can witness to what belief in God brings to life. A living faith animates human life and produces good fruit.

Explicit proclamation

Witness by itself is not enough. Witness must be followed by the verbal testimony to faith, or what Pope John Paul spoke of as "explicit proclamation". In *Redemptoris Missio* he pointed out: "Proclamation is the permanent priority of mission. The Church cannot elude Christ's explicit mandate, nor deprive men and women of the 'Good News' about their being loved and saved by God."

He quotes from Pope Paul: "Evangelisation will always contain – as the foundation, center and at the same time the summit of its dynamism – a clear proclamation that, in Jesus Christ ... salvation is offered to all people, as a gift of God's grace and mercy." Then he adds: "All forms of missionary activity are directed to this proclamation, which reveals and gives access to the mystery hidden for ages and made known in Christ (cf. Eph 3:3-9; Col 1:25-29), the mystery which lies at the heart of the Church's mission and life, as the hinge on which all evangelization turns."

In other words, the new evangelisation cannot be limited to witness. Indeed, the explicit expression of our faith is of vital importance.

7

Keys to the New Evangelisation

We can ask ourselves about the actual content of the message of the Church to the people of our time. This is a critical question. People today can be so far away from the Church and have little if any understanding of what Christianity is about. Our starting point in discussion or presentation of Christianity may be quite a distance from the kernel of the message. However, we need to know where we are going with our presentation of the Catholic faith.

As has been mentioned, the focus for the new evangelisation is Jesus Christ. We have already referred to the statements of both Pope John Paul II and Pope Benedict XVI who issued the call to "open the doors to Christ".

Pope Benedict developed this theme in a particular way and spoken on a number of occasions about the importance of developing a "personal relationship with Jesus":

> Christianity is not a new philosophy or new morality. We are Christians only if we encounter Christ ... Only in this personal relationship with Christ, only in this encounter with the Risen One do we really become Christians ... Therefore, let us pray to the Lord to enlighten us, so that, in our world, he will grant us the encounter with his presence, and thus give us a lively faith, an open heart, and great charity for all, capable of renewing the world.[70]

He saw that the task of the Church is to enable people to discover Jesus Christ in a personal way: "The evangelisation of the person and

---

70 Pope Benedict XVI, Vatican City, 3 September 2008.

of human communities depends totally on this encounter with Jesus Christ."[71] In *Deus Caritas Est* he stated: "Being Christian is not the result of an ethical choice or a lofty idea, but the encounter with an event, a person, which gives life a new horizon and a decisive direction."[72]

These examples can be multiplied. What is evident is that Pope Benedict was aware that the heart of what the Church has to offer the world is Jesus Christ.

The nature of faith

When we speak of a personal relationship with Christ we are conscious that this is only possible through faith. The nature of faith deserves particular attention. One of the great challenges we face today is the decline in faith in Western societies. Pope Benedict announced a Year of Faith to commence in October 2012. In his *Moto Proprio, Porta Fidei*, which he wrote to announce the Year of Faith, the he commented:

> To a greater extent than in the past, faith is now being subjected to a series of questions arising from a changed mentality which, especially today, limits the field of rational certainties to that of scientific and technological discoveries. Nevertheless the Church has never been afraid of demonstrating that there cannot be any conflict between faith and genuine science, because both, albeit by separate routes, tend towards the truth.[73]

He was conscious that the very notion of faith is under scrutiny today. Many with a scientific bent believe that the only source of knowledge is what can be scientifically verified. The question of faith is a subject that Pope Benedict addressed many times. He was aware

---

71 Pope Benedict XVI, Vatican City, 13 November 2007.
72 Pope Benedict XVI, *Deus Caritas Est* (2006), n. 1.
73 Pope Benedict XVI, *Porta Fidei*, n. 13.

that if faith in God is abandoned then humanity will be "impoverished, degraded and disfigured".[74]

He spoke in a very personal way about faith seeing it as the source of human happiness. In a Wednesday audience he said:

> In love, which seeks the good of the other, we find ourselves by giving ourselves away, in a process involving purification and healing of our hearts. So too in friendship, in the experience of beauty and the thirst for truth and goodness: we sense that we are caught up in a process which points us beyond ourselves to a mystery in which we dimly perceive the promise of complete fulfilment. Thanks to this innate sense, we can open our hearts to the gift of faith which draws us ever closer to God, the source of all good and the fulfilment of our deepest desire.[75]

Faith, for Pope Benedict, was the questing of the human heart for the divine. He was confident that faith is possible for every human being precisely because it is in our very nature. However, faith is not just a longing for the divine it has a quite specific nature in Christianity and that nature is connected intimately with a personal living relationship with the one who is the revelation of God and the path to union with him – Jesus Christ.

In the end, faith is a discovery of Jesus Christ who is the "Way to the Father."[76] The invisible God is made visible in Jesus Christ.

The *General Directory on Catechesis*, produced in 1998, describes what faith is in these words:

> The Christian faith is, above all, conversion to Jesus Christ, full and sincere adherence to his person and the decision to

---
74 Pope Benedict XVI, General Audience, 17 October 2012.
75 Pope Benedict XVI, General Audience, 7 November 2012.
76 John 14:6.

walk in his footsteps. Faith is a personal encounter with Jesus Christ making of oneself a disciple of him. This demands a permanent commitment to think like him, to judge like him and to live as he lived. In this way the believer unites himself to the community of disciples and appropriates the faith of the Church.[77]

Faith involves a response of the person to God both in the heart and in the mind. The Vatican Council document on Divine Revelation, *Dei Verbum*, had this to say on the nature of faith: "By faith man freely commits his entire self completely to God, making the full submission of his intellect and will to God who reveals, and willingly assenting to the Revelation given by him."[78]

Faith involves the giving over of one's entire self to God. This is a big ask today. We live in an age where people want to control their own destiny. They want to be in the driver's seat. To come to faith is quite counter-cultural.

Transformation through faith

Coming to faith results in a transformation of one's life. The General Directory paints a picture of the person who fully responds to Christ. This is our goal as Catholics:

Faith involves a change of life, a *metanoia*, that is a profound transformation of mind and heart; it causes the believer to live that conversion. This transformation of life manifests itself at all levels of the Christian's existence: in his interior life of adoration and acceptance of the divine will, in his action, participation in the mission of the Church, in his married and family life; in his professional life; in fulfilling economic and social responsibilities.[79]

---

77 *General Directory for Catechesis*, n. 53.
78 *Dei Verbum*, n. 5.
79 *General Directory for Catechesis*, n. 55.

The *General Directory* describes the coming to faith is a rather beautiful passage:

> Faith and conversion arise from the *"heart"*, that is, they arise from the depth of the human person and they involve all that he is. By meeting Jesus Christ and by adhering to him the human being sees all of his deepest aspirations completely fulfilled. He finds what he had always been seeking and he finds it superabundantly. Faith responds to that *"waiting"*, often unconscious and always limited in its knowledge of the truth about God, about man himself and about the destiny that awaits him. It is like pure water which refreshes the journey of man, wandering in search of his home. Faith is a gift from God. It can only be born in the intimacy of Man's heart as a fruit of that "grace [which] moves and assists him", and as a completely free response to the promptings of the Holy Spirit who moves the heart and turns it toward God, and who "makes it easy for all to accept and believe the truth".[80]

To explore this question further we need to examine two fundamental Christian concepts: salvation and grace. These are basic to the Christian mystery. Without an understanding of these two realities the new evangelisation will not have the requisite power to transform people's lives.

Salvation

Jesus, St John teaches, came not to condemn the world but so that through him the world might be saved.[81] Christianity is all about salvation. Jesus came to save us.

---

80 Ibid.
81 See *John* 3:17.

For the modern secularist this has no meaning. Many today consider it as an irrelevant question, especially if they have no clear sense of an afterlife. Many today would consider themselves basically good people and don't see any need for salvation.

The issue of salvation is a key issue today for the new evangelisation. It is something that many Catholics struggle to understand.

Many people today think they can manage their lives by themselves. When they examine their lives they think that they are doing okay. As long as life is running fairly well, there are a few moments of joy and celebration, people can tend to be content with their lot and the question of the need to be saved is largely an irrelevant question. If sooner or later things begin to go wrong they cannot relate to the idea of turning for help from God. Sadly some people live life as a constant struggle and cannot see any way out.

After all, society encourages us to have a positive attitude towards ourselves. The current view is that we should often be complimented for doing well. We live in a society which is oriented to positive affirmation. This is in reaction to the view that a previous age (Victorian) was judgemental and demanding. It is, of course, important to receive and give encouragement, but we cannot allow the practice to give a false view of life. We all need at times to be told honestly of our weaknesses and failures. At times we need to take stock of ourselves and acknowledge that there are some serious issues in our lives that we need to address.

In this climate we have witnessed the rise of the positive thinking gurus and "life coaches" who will convince us that we have all we need to be successful human beings. Their message is that I can make it with a little positive self-talk! It seems true and good at the time. Many get hyped up on self-talk and go out and think they can conquer the world. Sadly many come crashing down or simply find that things don't work out the way they had hoped.

Still many people seem to manage life reasonably well. They fail to see why they need to be saved. If life is viewed in terms of this world alone then salvation is not needed.

It is when we consider the reality of eternity that a different perspective is presented. Eternity gives a real orientation to life. Without a consideration of life after death, the attitude that a person should attempt to get the best out of life makes sense.

Facing judgement

If a person does believe in eternal life, they possibly realise that they one day they will have to face the judgement seat of God.

Let us imagine this for a moment. The end of life has come and each person must present themselves before the judgement seat of God. Many today would be quietly confident. They would consider that they have led a reasonably good life and can expect a favourable judgement.

Let us further imagine the scene that is often understood in popular mind. God will open the Book of Life. He will look up the person's name. Many see the Book of Life as a ledger – there is a credit page and a debit page. There will be a few items on the debit page – no-one is perfect! But most people will wait till God looks at the credit page. People think of all the good things they have done. If it were an exam they reckon they could achieve a mark of a minimum of 60-70 per cent. Anyway, they think, 50 per cent should get me over the line!

Is that how it works? Can we gain heaven because we have earned it? Do we deserve eternal life with God because we have been led a reasonably good life? Can I stand before the pearly gates and say, "God here I am let me in I have earned the right to heaven"?

This view is quite common, even if it is not articulated in the form above. Many today believe that eternal life is to be earned. However, life is a gift from God. Eternal life is a gift from God. We did not decide to be born. God gave us life and breathed an eternal soul into each of us. When death comes, we are completely powerless. We cannot control what will happen to us. We are completely in the hands of God.

We cannot save ourselves.

Realising we need to be saved

This question of salvation is a difficult one for the modern mind. Yet it is a critical element to the Christian message, and hence to the new evangelisation. We need to preach about salvation.

As a young priest I remember once talking about this to a group of young people and raising the issue of our need to be saved, arguing that we cannot save ourselves. One student – an architecture student – couldn't accept my thesis. He was convinced that he could save himself by virtue of the life he chose to live. Next weekend he went surfing. He was a good swimmer. He got caught in a rip and was swept out. And to his embarrassment he had to be rescued. Somewhat chastened he spoke to me privately afterwards and said that he now understood why we need to be saved: even though he was a good swimmer, he got caught in something which was more powerful than he was, and he needed someone to come out and save him.

In the face of death we are powerless. In terms of eternity it is God's gift to us by virtue of his mercy and not something we can claim for ourselves.

How are we saved?

To be saved we need to surrender ourselves into the hands of God. The young architectural student needed to allow the surf lifesaver to rescue him. To do this he needed to surrender himself into the hands of the lifesaver. He had to stop trying by his own effort and let the lifesaver take over.

Salvation requires a surrender of ourselves, particularly our will. This is something very difficult for the contemporary generations who have grown up with a sense of capacity to manage their own lives. Living in affluence, having a good education, having access to good health care, and enjoying many opportunities for a good life, the notion of surrender is something that is quite alien.

Once staying in Rome I met a young Australian lawyer who was working in London. The lawyer asked to be shown around Rome. So we visited various places around Rome. I proposed that we meet some good friends of mine – all of whom were dead. They were the saints buried in Rome. So we visited a number of tombs of saints – St Peter, St Paul, St Catherine of Sienna, St Monica, St Agnes, and others.

Later in the day we visited the tomb of St Ignatius Loyola in the Church of the Gesu and on the kneeler in front of his tomb was his great prayer that is now particularly known as the Catholic hymn: "Take Lord Receive", a hymn composed by the St Louis Jesuits.

It is a wonderful prayer. St Ignatius gives it at a special moment in his *Spiritual Exercises*:

> Take, O Lord, and receive my entire liberty,
> my memory, my understanding and my whole will.
> All that I am and all that I possess You have given me.
> I surrender it all to You to be disposed of according to
> Your will.

> Give me only Your love and Your grace;
> with these I will be rich enough,
> and will desire nothing more.

This young lawyer had a problem with it. Why would you want to pray this? Isn't this a denial of personal freedom and self-determination?

It is hard to explain to young people today the need to surrender ourselves and our lives to Christ. It goes against the grain for generation Y. They have been brought up on affirmation. They have been told that they can make their own future.

But this is an essential element to the Christian message. Without grasping its essential truth a person cannot come into the fullness of the Christian mystery. Without some degree of surrender, the grace of God is inhibited.

St Paul understood this truth so well:

> Whatever gains I had, these I have come to consider a loss because of Christ. More than that, I even consider everything as a loss because of the supreme good of knowing Christ Jesus my Lord. For his sake I have accepted the loss of all things and I consider them so much rubbish, that I may gain Christ and be found in him, not having any righteousness of my own based on the law but that which comes through faith in Christ, the righteousness from God, depending on faith to know him and the power of his resurrection and [the] sharing of his sufferings by being conformed to his death, if somehow I may attain the resurrection from the dead (Philippians 3:7-11).

St Paul understood that in the end it is God's mercy that saves me and all he wanted was to be so united with him while on earth that Christ will raise him up and bring him into the Kingdom of his Father.

The words of Jesus on the cross: "Into your hands I commend my spirit" expresses this reality. At the end of our life this is all we can do and what we should do. This is the way in which each Christian can die. This can be the final prayer on our lips as we sink into the mystery of death. We surrender ourselves to the loving mercy of God.

Walking on water

A Gospel story which fittingly captures this issue of surrender is that of St Peter walking on the water. It is a well-known story told by St Matthew (Matthew 14:22-33).

The disciples were in the boat out on the lake. Jesus remained behind after the miracle of feeding the 5,000. A storm blows up as evening came. Jesus came to them walking on the lake. They are terrified – it is a ghost they say. Jesus immediately says to them: "Take courage! It is I. Do not be afraid." Peter then says, "Lord, if it's you, tell me to come to you on the water." Jesus says, "Come." Peter got down out of the boat, walked on the water and came toward Jesus. Then he saw the wind, he was afraid and, beginning to sink, he cried out, "Lord, save me!" Jesus reached out his hand and caught him. "You man of little faith," he said, "why did you doubt?"

This story can be the story of our life and of our death. The Lord invites us to come to him – finally through death. But now as we live our lives Jesus calls us to entrust ourselves to him. While our eyes are fixed on him all is well. If trouble comes, he will be there to save us.

A little postscript: one often hears of the question posed by evangelicals: "Are you saved?" It can be a confusing question to answer. Do I answer yes or no? Fundamentally, it is a false question. The Catholic response to such a question is: I have been saved through the death of Christ on the cross, I am being saved by the action of the Holy Spirit in my life and I hope to be finally saved by the Mercy of God.

Grace

The other question which is very important in the new evangelisation is that of Grace. Once again the notion of Grace is a difficult one for people to grasp. Indeed many Catholics struggle with the concept.

As Catholics we are very good about *doing*. The Catholic Church is very active. We have many diverse organisations which provide education, healthcare, welfare and charity. We can be justifiably proud of our wide range of activities inspired by our Catholic faith. We are busy about doing many things as the Lord commented to Martha. However, I think that we are not so good at *being*. We are aware that it is who we *are* that gives life and vitality to what we *do*.

Thus, it is the quality of our inner life of faith – our relationship with God in Jesus Christ – that should be the source of what animates all that we do in and through the Church. If this is lacking then we may do what is required of us, but its spiritual potential will be severely limited. Over time the works will be more humanistic or even simply bureaucratic. This was the concern reflected by Pope Benedict in *Deus Caritas Est* when he commented: "It is very important that the Church's charitable activity maintains all of its splendour and does not become just another form of social assistance".[82]

Contemporary Pelagianism

Many Catholics believe that we save ourselves by our good works. This is also the view that many evangelicals have of the Catholic Church. St Paul taught that we are "saved by grace through faith"? For many today this is a mysterious statement.

In his letter to the Ephesians St Paul says, "For it is by grace you

---

82 *Deus Caritas Est*, n. 31.

have been saved, through faith – and this is not from yourselves, it is the gift of God – not by works, so that no-one can boast" (Ephesians 2, 8-9). St Paul emphasised a key understanding about the nature of salvation that we are saved by grace and not by works.

On this matter it is useful to revisit the teaching of St Augustine of Hippo who is called the "Doctor of Grace". He wrote on the subject of grace in answer to the teaching of the fourth century British monk, Pelagius. Pelagius emphasised human freedom and will as the key to living the Christian life. In other words, Pelagius believed we could save ourselves by our own effort. St Augustine strongly challenged this view.

In his *Confessions* as he reflects on his own life St Augustine says, "all my hope is nothing except in Your great mercy", and then adds in prayerful thanks to God, "it is only by Your grace and mercy that You have melted away the ice of my evil". St Augustine understood in the light of his experience that it is God gives us the power to respond to him. He says, "You commanded me ... and since you gave me the power, it was so done." He understood that grace prefaces and enables all good actions.

Many today do not appreciate the importance of grace in the Christian life. As we have said, many today tend to think that they can manage by ourselves. They think that they can save themselves by their own efforts. We often hear people say: "I will try to lead a good life". This was what Pelagius proposed. His teaching is still very much alive today. This is a blind spot in the minds of many Catholics and to grasp the nature of grace will help the Church be more effective in the new evangelisation.

St Paul and St Augustine would say quite definitively that we cannot save ourselves. St Paul summed up what the Christian life is in these words, "We are all God's work of art" (Ephesians 2:1), that is, the good in us is solely the fruit of God's action in our lives. We must co-operate, yes, but the fruit is God's work and not ours.

Explaining grace

How can we explain grace? Its meaning eludes many today.

A way in which grace can be understood is that it is a little like breathing. We do not often think about the fact that we breathe, but it is vital to our staying alive. So too grace, which is the Holy Spirit, initiates and sustains our faith and spiritual life. St Paul said that we cannot even say "Jesus is Lord" without the action of the Holy Spirit (see I Corinthians 12:3). Thus, just because we do not allude to the action of the Holy Spirit it does not mean He is not active within us.

St Thomas Aquinas comments on this matter in these words:

> Now there are five effects of grace in us: of these, the first is to heal the soul; the second, to desire good; the third, to carry into effect the good proposed; the fourth, to persevere in good; the fifth, to reach glory.[83]

He teaches here that grace precedes any good action, enables it to take place and produces the fruit from the action. Such is the nature of the Christian life. We do not have to struggle alone in our quest for goodness and holiness.

This is what the Christian life has to offer. It is a life of Grace. God is an active agent in our growth. This is the good news which the Church has to offer the world today. This is one of the treasures of the faith that can give power and efficacy to the new evangelisation.

---

83 *De Natura et Gracia*, xxxi.

Divine Providence

One aspect of the notion of Grace that does not receive much attention today is that of the role of Divine Providence. The saints understood this well. They knew that they were part of a greater plan. Their lives were not simply the product of their own effort but rather God played an active role and would be an agent in their life and mission. They learnt to rely upon Divine Providence because of their conviction of being caught up in the Divine Plan.

A prayer of St Jane Francis de Chantal captures this:

> Therefore I resolve with your Divine assistance, O my Saviour, to follow your desires and your ordinances, without regarding or examining why you do this rather than that; but I will blindly follow you according to your Divine will, without seeking my own inclinations.

The Catholic spiritual tradition has a lively sense of trust in Divine Providence. Saints were only too aware of their own frailty and readily abandoned themselves to the wisdom and grace of God. The saints were aware that we are totally dependent on grace. They understood that grace is everything.

It is God who sustains each of us in being. We cannot "make" ourselves alive. We did not will ourselves into existence. We cannot control the ultimate path each of us must take as we approach death. St Paul said to the Greek philosophers on the Areopagus, "In God we live and move and have our being" (Acts 17:28). So it is true that the spiritual dimension to our lives is sustained by grace. Our faith, our good works, all are the fruit of grace.

8

Preaching the New Evangelisation

Having considered some of the key elements of the content of the message in the new evangelisation we will consider how the component elements can be assembled into a basic kerygma for the contemporary context. We should note that while the essential message is the same, its presentation by Jesus and then by the first Christians has to be seen within the particular context of the times. In our times the message has to be tailored to meet the real needs of people.

The word, kerygma, is a transliteration of the Greek word that means proclamation or preaching. Depending on the context, it may refer to either the content proclaimed or the act of proclaiming. It refers to preaching or proclaiming, as distinct from teaching or instruction (*didache*) in the Gospel of Christ. It is worth recalling that before the Gospel was written, it was first preached (Romans 16:25).

The actual content of proclamation, while essentially the same, has some variant expression according to circumstances. Thus for instance, there is the kerygma of John the Baptist who saw his task of preparing for the coming of the Messiah. He particularly called on people to repent and to express this by a washing in the River Jordan. Turning from sin and preparing oneself to welcome the Messiah was at the heart of the preaching of the Baptist.

When we come to examine the preaching of Jesus we note that Jesus began his public ministry with the simple message: "Repent and believe for the Kingdom of God is close at hand." God's Kingdom is amongst the people and in order to receive the grace of God one needs to enter into belief by the way of repentance. Jesus began his public ministry by building on the preaching of St John the Baptist. Of course, he would take it much further as he explained the nature of the Kingdom of God by his parables. Jesus highlighted the need for humility as a necessary basis to receive what God has in store for those who accept Jesus.

On Pentecost morning St Peter preached the Resurrection of Christ and urged his listeners to repent of their sins and be baptised. They would receive the gift of the Holy Spirit by accepting Jesus as Lord and Saviour.

Finally as we turn to St Paul we notice that he understood the significance of the death of Christ. In the cross of Christ is found the power and wisdom of God. St Paul knew that the kerygma is not human eloquence or wisdom. Those who accept this kerygma do so because the power of the Holy Spirit touches their hearts.

While we can see a variety of approaches to the kerygma, there is one central truth and one Gospel (Good News): Jesus Christ has come to save us and this has been achieved through his death and resurrection. Accepting this means that one turns to God acknowledges ones sin and receives the power of God into their lives.

Basic components of the Christian kerygma can be identified. As we enter the third millennium and engage particularly in the task of the new evangelisation we can identify a number of key elements that make up the kerygma. They can be listed as follows:

- God is love.
- Repentance.
- Jesus the Saviour.

- Decision.
- Life of Grace.
- Members of the Body of Christ.

We will examine each of them in turn and consider how they can be presented in the contemporary culture.

i. God is love

One cannot presume that today people have an understanding that God is a God of love. Those with a minimal contact with Christianity may have a sense of some divine power, but their understanding of the nature of God may be clouded by beliefs from other religions like Buddhism or by the New Age.

A good starting point is the well-known statement in St John's Gospel: "For God so loved the world, that he gave his only Son, that whoever believes in him should not perish but have eternal life" (John 3:16). It is one of the most quoted texts of the Scriptures. It summarises the meaning of the coming of Jesus Christ and declares some fundamental Christian truths.

The first truth that it proclaims is that God has acted out of love. God is love, St John reminds us (I John 4:8). All God's actions are the expression of his love. God choose to create the world as an act of love. Love cannot contain itself. It wants to create. Love gives life. This love is such that it gives without demanding return.

This explanation that God is love can be continued by the consideration that God could have made all creation such that it was completely subservient to him. He could have made human beings like robots. Robots would obey what was asked of them but they cannot love. Love is freely given and love lets the other be free. God has created human beings free. We are free to respond to the love of God or choose not to.

The second fundamental Christian truth is that God so loved the world that he sent his only Son to assume our condition and live among us. This is a truth that is beyond human reckoning. God did not just send a prophet (which he had done), or a great spiritual leader (he did inspire various great leaders), but in the end he chose to send his own beloved Son.

The parable of the landowner of the vineyard (Matthew 21:33-43) is illustrative. The landowner initially sent his servants to collect the rent. His servants were rejected. Finally he sent his Son. "They will respect my Son", he said hopefully. God the Father has so much concern for us that he was prepared to "risk" his only Son.

The third truth revealed in this text is that the reason that God acted in this way was that people may have eternal life. Jesus became man for this one reason – that humans might be able to share eternal life with God, the creatures united for eternity with their Creator. This reveals what God desires for us above all else. God wants us to be with him forever. In particular God wants to enable us to share in his joy and life. This what God wants for us. God wants to share heavenly glory with us. "Come and share your master's happiness" (Matthew 25:23), Jesus said in one of his parables. This is what God longs to offer us.

These truths need to be presented as a basis to our proclamation. People need to come to grasp the extraordinary nature of God.

The next line of the Johannine text is: "For God did not send his Son into the world to condemn the world, but in order that the world might be saved through him." The act of God was not an act of judgement and condemnation, but rather an act of mercy aimed at saving humanity. The parable of the Prodigal Son which is really the parable of the Forgiving Father captures strikingly the heart of God the Father and his single desire for the wellbeing of his son.

In the parable the father waited, he looked down the road in hope and expectation that he would see his returning son. Then one day the son appeared. Jesus tells us that the father ran to embrace the boy. There were no words of condemnation and judgement. There is only the expression of forgiveness and mercy. He was welcomed home. This is revelation of the heart of God. This is what is in the heart of God for humanity, for sinful humanity.

It is possible to follow this line of thought to its conclusion when we consider the means by which we were saved. The text we have been quoting is part of the conversation between the Lord and a Pharisee named Nicodemus who came to Jesus secretly by night. The Lord declared to Nicodemus, "just as Moses lifted up the serpent in the wilderness, so must the Son of Man be lifted up, that whoever believes in him may have eternal life".

The reference to "lifted up" is a reference to the crucifixion as Jesus was raised up on a cross. Thus the full meaning of the text is clear – God loves the world so much that he will send his own Son who will die on a cross to save us.

The great symbol of our Catholic faith is the crucifix. The crucifix has a prominent place in our churches. It is often atop our Catholic buildings – not only our churches, but our presbyteries, our schools, our hospitals. It is found in our homes. It is on our rosary beads. We wear it around our necks. It is the greatest of all the symbols of the Christian faith.

The cross is an instrument of death and yet it is the predominant image used by Christianity. Our primary symbol is that of a dying man. However when we look at a crucifix what do we see? Do we shudder at viewing this cruel inhuman instrument of torture? Do we look with pity on a dying man?

We look beyond what our eyes behold. We know what the cross is and we behold a man dying, but we see something far more than this. When we look at a crucifix we are gazing on the Son of God. We know too why he is on the cross. We know why he accepted such suffering. We know the purposes of his Father in heaven in asking this of him.

When we look on a crucifix we see love. We can hear in our hearts the words from John 3:16 – "God so loved the world". To truly know the love of God for us there is no better thing to do that to gaze upon the cross. We can be like St John or the holy women and stand at the foot of the cross. In silence we can ponder this immense mystery – thus does God love humanity, thus does God love me.

The proclamation of the love of God is to proclaim that this love is personal for each one. So we can say with utter conviction, "I know God loves me". Many can't bring themselves to believe this. Perhaps they feel that they are not worthy of such love. It could be that their own lives have denied them of the experience of personal love and so they do not really know what it means. Or it may simply be that it is too much to think that God can be interested in me personally. It is one of the saddest things that some people think that they are beyond love.

This love is real and can be experienced. If a person has not experienced the love of God in a personal way then we can encourage them to ask this of the Lord: let me know your love.

The kerygma needs to begin at this place. What follows will build on this foundation. Without understanding the depth of the love of God for humanity and for each of us individually the call to repentance and to respond to what God has done will be difficult to understand and accept.

ii. Repentance

The kerygma needs to address the nature of sin in human life. This is not something that can be glossed over. The redemptive work of God in Christ only makes sense when we are able to confront the reality of our sinfulness. Sin is what separates us from God. Jesus came to redeem us from sin. The message of St Paul in his Letter to the Romans is that the Christian proclamation centres on the redemption from sin won for us by Christ.

For many today the issue of sin is a difficult one. Many find it hard to identify as a sinner and to see the need to come before God in humility and ask for forgiveness. Yet sin is the reality in every person's life. If we do not acknowledge that we are sinners then we do not see the need for God's mercy.

Jesus began his ministry with the call to turn away from sin and believe the Gospel. This must also be the call of the Church. It must be a subject dealt with if the evangelisation process is to be real.

Even if we do accept that we have sinned there is the tendency to minimise its seriousness. We readily make excuses for ourselves. We blame others or particular circumstances. It is tempting to prefer to forget our failings. People these days speak about "moving on with their lives". We try to put negative things behind us and move forward.

One of the issues we face today is that a sense of sin has been lost. One of the needs in the new evangelisation is to speak much more about the reality of sin.

If we have sinned then we have been marked by what we have done even if we dismiss its seriousness or try to move on from what we did. One image that can assist in understanding this is to imagine that each of us is carrying a backpack and every time we sin we pick up a rock and place it in our backpack; small rocks for small sins, big rocks for big sins. Gradually as sins mount the weight becomes greater. Sins happen and they become part of our history and part of us. We cannot ignore that they have occurred. What is important is that we deal with them.

Then we need to point out that there is a way to deal with our sins. We need to approach the Lord and ask for forgiveness.

As Jesus was dying on the cross we are told that at one time he cried out, "Father, forgive them, they know not what they do" (Luke 23:24). We can hear these words as referring to the cruel soldiers who nailed him there, or applying to the Jewish leaders and all those who cried out "crucify him", but we can also hear these words as words referring to us.

Why was Jesus dying on the cross? It was for us, for our sins, for the sins of humanity. So his prayer to the Father was his great cry for all of humanity: "Father forgive them, they do not know what they are doing".

When we look up at the cross we can hear the Lord pleading on our behalf – "Father forgive him/her". And we when we look up at the cross we can think – Jesus had done this because of my sins. Our prayer gazing up on the crucified Christ can be: "Jesus, you did this for me. You did this for me because of my sins."

The proclamation of the Gospel must include a call to people to walk the path of repentance and find forgiveness. This path is the path to freedom, to healing and to new life in God's Holy Spirit.

God longs to bring us into the fullness of his own life. However we are sinners. We are fragile and imperfect. We are far from God.

In order that the power and love of God can transform us we must follow the path of growing in a humble and contrite heart and through repentance allow God's grace to purify us and raise us up in holiness of life.

The path of repentance is the path to grace. The path of repentance is the path to the healing of our hearts. The path of repentance is the path to joy, to freedom and to new life. This message is not easy to present but once grasped leads people to the freedom of being able to unburden their lives.

How can we raise the issue of sin and repentance in such a way that people can receive our message and respond? A starting point can be the story of the adulterous woman brought to Jesus (John 7:58-8:11).

In this story we are given a glimpse of what lies in the heart of Jesus as he was confronted with the woman caught in adultery. Her accusers demand cold hard justice: death by stoning.

The response of Jesus was not to join their condemnation nor present a counter accusation of their own cold heartedness. Rather he moved to silence – as he would move to silence when he himself was accused before Pilate. In the heat and emotion of accusation – particularly accusation fuelled by jealousy as it Jesus' case – silence brings a calm and clarity.

From the silence came a response that reduced the accusers to their own silence. Jesus spoke the truth with such convicting force that one by one we are told those who sought vindictive condemnation withdrew.

His simple statement emerging from the silence has entered our cultural imagination: "Let he who is without sin cast the first stone." None of us can stand in judgement and condemnation of another. It is expressed at the popular level by the saying, those who live in glass houses shouldn't throw stones.

In the heart of Jesus was the desire to grant mercy and forgiveness. He sent the woman away with the simple instruction to sin no more. She would have known her sin as she was confronted publicly with it. She would have known the shame of this public humiliation. She would have feared for the consequences of her actions by a death by stoning.

In the midst of her seemingly hopeless situation she experienced mercy coming from Jesus. She had her life restored not only physically, but also morally and spiritually. This act of mercy would have been a power of love flowing through her that would inspire her to live differently. Her spirit was touched and with the words "sin no more" residing within her she would have had the capacity now to change her life.

Such is the power of forgiveness. It not only wipes away the sin but restores the inner spirit. Sin cripples our spirit. Sin weighs down on our soul. Sin fosters defeatism and a sense that all is beyond redemption. We say to ourselves that we cannot change. We resign ourselves to the conviction that this is how I am. The devil – "the accuser of the brethren" – uses sin as one of his great tools to sap our hope and convince us that we cannot change. We wallow in our failure and weakness.

When we do not approach Christ in the Sacrament of Penance we remain caught up in our sin. We resign ourselves to mediocrity. We continue through life crippled and defeated. In this the devil has won a victory over us and he can lock us off from hope and change.

Mercy heals the soul. Mercy breathes new hope and life into us. The experience of mercy reinvigorates our spirit.

In the heart of Jesus is mercy not condemnation. In the heart of

Jesus is a desire to forgive and so revive our spirits. In the heart of Jesus lives the desire that we change and grow and come to holiness and human flourishing.

God is a god of life and salvation.

iii. Jesus the Saviour

We have already spoken extensively on the theme of salvation. This message stands is stark contrast to the message of the world around us. The secularism, individualism and relativism of our day form mindsets which are serious barriers to a person coming to accept salvation through Jesus Christ. This is why this critical message which is the heart of evangelisation needs to be preceded by the two previous proclamations of the love of God and the need for repentance. A person who is moving along the lines proposed by the earlier presentations will be more likely to understand and embrace the message of salvation found in Jesus Christ.

As we saw, many today consider that we save ourselves and earn the right to heaven. The picture we painted standing before the judgement seat of God and the Book of Life is opened is in the minds of many. Even people of deep faith imagine that the Book of Life is like a book of accounts with a debit page and a credit page and many good people are quietly confident that in the end the credits will far outweigh the debits and that we will hear the words, "well done good and faithful servant". They will feel that they have rightly earned a place in heaven.

A person who sees things thus will try to achieve goodness by their own efforts. By doing this they limit or prevent the action of divine grace in their lives. It is like choosing to get to the top of a tall building by using the stairs rather than hopping on the elevator.

The heart of the kerygma is the proclamation that salvation is found in Jesus Christ. As St John never tired of saying: God sent his only Beloved Son so that through him the world might be saved. The Church presents Jesus Christ to the world and invites all to recognise him as the Son of God sent as our redeemer. Such a recognition of who Jesus is cannot be left as an intellectual truth to be accepted, but must become a profound conviction of the heart which calls forth an unqualified opening of the self to the salvation offered in Christ.

Preaching such a message can take various concrete forms. We have noted many of them already.

One concrete form is that proposed by popes John Paul II and Benedict XVI when they invited people to *"open the doors to Christ"*. This expression is a very appropriate contemporary formula. Modern people understand its personalist language. The Scripture passage underpinning it from the Book of Revelations 3:20 and it carries the respect God has for our human freedom. Jesus knocks and waits for a response. He does not impose or force himself on a person. He desires to share himself with them but will wait upon their response. This image can well be used to assist people in understanding what is asked of them.

The difficulty that this approach may present to people today is that it threatens personal integrity: if I open my life to Christ will I lose control of my life? Pope Benedict reassured us that this would not happen but it can be daunting to many today who so prize their human freedom. Pope John Paul before him encouraged people to respond saying, in a favourite phrase of his, "do not be afraid". Both Popes knew that people today have a reluctance to entrust their lives to anyone or anything.

A second form which is an extension of this invitation is one of *giving over one's heart to Christ*. Such language can readily resonate with people today. The world around us, particularly through advertising, emphasises the value of doing things for personal advantage. In one way or another the message we constantly hear is that "this is for the most important person in the world: you". Christianity proposes the polar opposite. The Gospel teaching of Jesus highlights this. He says, "Unless you deny yourself and take up your cross you cannot be my disciple" (Matthew 16:24). Jesus speaks of the man who builds bigger and bigger barns only to find that an account will be asked of his life (Luke 12:15-21). The story of the rich young man speaks of the dangers of possessions limiting our freedom to give ourselves generously to Christ (Luke 18:18-23).

Sometimes this approach is summarised by a diagram depicting our life, with ourselves at the centre and Jesus as one of many other competing influences. Another diagram presents the Christian as one who has allowed Jesus to become the centre of their life. This depiction may be quite challenging for many today. People today want to determine their own lives and futures. Many would find it difficult to surrender their freedom in this way. Pope Benedict addressed this modern fear in his first homily as Pope:

> Are we not perhaps all afraid in some way? If we let Christ enter fully into our lives, if we open ourselves totally to him, are we not afraid that He might take something away from us? Are we not perhaps afraid to give up something significant, something unique, something that makes life so beautiful? Do we not then risk ending up diminished and deprived of our freedom? ... No! If we let Christ into our lives, we lose nothing, nothing, absolutely nothing of what makes life free, beautiful and great. No! Only in this friendship are the doors of life opened wide. Only in this friendship is the great potential of human existence truly revealed. Only in

this friendship do we experience beauty and liberation. And so, today, with great strength and great conviction, on the basis of long personal experience of life, I say to you, dear young people: Do not be afraid of Christ! He takes nothing away, and he gives you everything. When we give ourselves to him, we receive a hundredfold in return. Yes, open, open wide the doors to Christ – and you will find true life. Amen.

Jesus himself comments on this theme when he says that he who loses his life for my sake will find it (Matthew 16:25).

There is a profound truth here which many today find hard to grasp. Giving over our lives to Jesus is not a loss of freedom but the actual enhancing of our freedom. It is not a denial of our right to self-determination but can be the very means by which our destiny is transformed. The miracle of the changing of the water into wine is a parable of how the blessing of Jesus over our lives can transform our ordinariness into something extraordinary. The stories of the lives of saints give great witness to this truth.

Another way to approach this question of response to Christ is that of *discipleship*. The Gospels record that Jesus called his disciples to "come follow me". This call invited them to orient their lives around him and to place themselves under his direction. The relationship between Jesus and his disciples was one of master/disciple. The disciple is one who sits at the feet of the master and listens. The notion of being willing to be formed by Jesus can be a useful way of presenting the meaning of being a Christian.

Once again it presents a very different concept of human living. The society around us proposes that we become the masters of our own destiny. The words of the Frank Sinatra song – "I did it my way" – resonate so readily with people today. The world proposes that we should think for ourselves and formulate our own set of principles and values. The relativist tenor of our time proposes that we adopt a critical stance and only accept those notions that we can accept according to our own lights and understanding. It is a cafeteria approach to life. In a cafeteria we choose what we want or like and pass over those things which are not to our taste. Christianity proposes a full submission to the teaching and example of Jesus Christ and thence of his Church. This is a tall order for people today. Yet it is the path to inner freedom.

The downside of this presentation is that people will consider that life will become boring and predictable. People will be fearful that their own self-realisation will be denied. What will God ask of me?, they wonder. Yet there is another truth that is often played out in people's lives today: If we stand for nothing we will fall for everything.

A fourth approach that is finding its way into the teaching of Pope Benedict and which can be better received by the modern mind is that of forming *a personal relationship with Jesus Christ*. This is the age of forming relationships. The popularity of various forms of social media and the constant use of mobile phones to be in contact with people highlights the desire for relationships. Christianity can be presented as the manifestation of the desire of God to be in relationship with us. St John describes Jesus as the Word made flesh – that is, the communication of God to us. Jesus is the communication of God with humanity realised in human form. Psalm 139 with its emphasis on the intimate personal knowledge that God has of us can assist people in grasping that God is personally interested in each one of us. Jesus himself in the ways in which he related so personally with all sorts of people gives testimony to the desire of God to enter into a personal relationship with us. The path for that relationship is Jesus himself. He who sees me sees the Father.

It is possible to present this avenue as a means of coming to personal faith. This approach highlights the dignity of each individual. Each person is respected in their own right. This is attractive to people today.

A possible downside to this approach is that people may treat it too lightly, seeing God as being weak in accepting us so readily and asking little of us. It can create a sense of an easy familiarity which can breed contempt, as the saying goes. The demands of the Gospel can be overlooked, the sense of sin dismissed and the expectations of a change in the direction of life ignored. However, having said that, such a path can lead a person along the way to a deeper understanding of the Christian mystery. Some are simply not ready for a major reshaping of their lives when they first come to hear the Gospel message and a simple do-able step can allow them to enter on a path that will lead them deeper into the Christian life.

One other approach that is faithful to the deepest meaning of the coming of Christ is to present *the mystery of the cross*. In this approach the evangelist focuses upon Christ crucified. The emphasis can be an invitation to see in the crucified Christ the ultimate expression of the depth of the love of God for humanity. God the Father was prepared to sacrifice his own beloved Son so that humanity may be redeemed. This approach allows for the presentation of the sinful condition of humanity expressed so clearly in St Paul's Letter to the Romans. It allows for an explanation of the central mystery recalled and proclaimed at every Mass: we proclaim your death O Lord and profess your resurrection.

The response that such a presentation demands is the invitation to accept that Jesus died for us. We understand that we should gratefully and humbly accept this salvation.

The downside to this approach is that the language surrounding this profound mystery is beyond the grasp of many today. Redemption, salvation, satisfaction for our sins, atonement are all very difficult concepts for people of today to grasp.

In whatever form the preaching of salvation in Jesus Christ is presented, it is important that there is an opportunity for the hearers to respond. They must not just look at the mirror and walk away as St James warns.[84]

iv. Making a decision

After hearing the preaching of St Peter at Pentecost, his listeners asked, "What must we do brothers?" When a person is convinced by the presentation of the Gospel they know that a response is called for. The Gospel is such that it is not something that can be accepted as useful information or even a code of behaviour. The Gospel is such that it requires a complete personal response. The place of response is the heart. One can be convinced intellectually but the place of response is not just in the head. While we are called upon to make a "religious assent" it is at the level of the heart – the centre of the entire person that a full and complete response will be made. St Luke says that they were "cut to the heart". This is the power of the Gospel and the response is to take place in the heart.

St Paul knew this. He described the Gospel in terms of power – the power of God to save. In Romans 1:16 he says, "For I am not ashamed of the Gospel, for it is God's power for salvation to everyone who believes." For the evangelist it is not enough just to present the message but to also lead people in a path of response. Again, this can take a variety of expressions.

Prior to discussing the ways in which a person can be led in a response it is worth commenting on the ways in which the faith

---

84 See James 1:23-25.

was transmitted in the immediate past. In times past there was a triumvirate of sources for the effective transmission of the Catholic faith from one generation to the next: the family, the parish and the Catholic school.

The family – the primary source for the nourishment of faith – was, in the past, a closer unit. Family life which reflected Catholic faith meant that children imbued the faith as the atmosphere of their lives. This faith was not questioned; it was accepted. Outside forces bearing in on the family were not as present in times past. Parents who prized the value of the faith readily taught it and urged their children to embrace it. Faith was received by a process of osmosis, it seeped into their souls. They accepted it as a natural part of their identity and in a society that was more marked along sectarian lines, Catholic young people considered their faith a badge of honour.

Similarly the parish offered a tangible expression to the faith. The local Catholic Church was clearly identifiable with its distinctive Catholic iconography – the stained glass windows, the Stations of the Cross, the statues and the tabernacle. Every time you entered the church you entered the Catholic world which was steeped in images of the transcendent world. The liturgical life expressed in its own language (Latin) and captured in hymns, incense and ancient prayers transported a person into another very different but very real world. The parish was replete with Catholic cultural images. It was clearly distinguishable from other expressions of Christianity and certainly from the world of other religions.

The Catholic school reinforced this cultural landscape and provided a systematic formation in this clearly definable world view. Prayers were said regularly during the day, visits to the Blessed Sacrament were encouraged and a sense of belonging to a particular spiritual tribe was constantly reinforced.

In this total environment the faith was "caught". It seeped into every aspect of life. It was a total package. To believe was presumed. This is essentially a process of spiritual osmosis rather than faith being born of personal conviction.

Today in such dramatically changed times this formula which was so successful for so long no longer works. Indeed there is a reverse osmosis. Faith is being drained out of the lives of people. Forces have invaded the family principally through the various forms of media. The parish is not viewed as attractive. It has become more a service centre than a vital community. The school environment today can even be antagonistic towards the serious commitment to living the Catholic faith.

Something new is required to counter this. That new thing is a call for a person to make an individual sincere decision to be a Catholic. Such a decision will be reached when the Gospel is presented in such a way that they see the need to decide to orient their lives around Jesus Christ. A person will make such a decision when they arrive at a moment in their lives when the clarity of the decision for Christ is evident and they desire no longer to live for themselves but for Christ. This simply is a moment of grace. It cannot be manufactured artificially, but when the moment comes the means to respond needs to be presented lest the person draw away in uncertainty as to what is needed of them.

Let us examine some of the paths that can be taken in this process of making a decision for Christianity. There is no one formula that is required for a person to embrace the Christian life. However what is important is that a step is proposed to them. When a person is moved by evangelical preaching it is important to give them a way in which they can express their desire to respond. Often the step proposed will be consistent with the approach taken in the preaching and will be a way that is appropriate to the person and the particular circumstances.

Some possible ways are offered below. This is not an exclusive list. There are many creative and appropriate ways in which a person can give expression to their desire to accept and embrace a new found relationship with God in Christ.

1. When St Peter was asked what his listeners were to do, he unhesitatingly said that they must be baptised. Obviously for those who have not been baptised this is the path that is recommended for them. The Church offers the RCIA as the pathway to entering into the life of the Church.

In some settings it may be appropriate as a form of response to receiving the Gospel message to invite already baptised people to renew their baptismal promises. Properly explained and solemnly performed, this can be a significant moment for a person to claim the full meaning of their baptism and resolve to live out their baptismal identity.

2. With the current rediscovery of the beauty and attractiveness of Adoration of the Blessed Sacrament, the use of exposition of the Blessed Sacrament can provide a powerful setting for the expression of a commitment to Jesus Christ. Accompanied by songs of worship and perhaps completed by a benediction, the strong spiritual atmosphere can draw forth a sincere act of re-orientation of life around Jesus Christ.

3. For many older Catholics not so accustomed to spontaneous acts of prayer, the use of hallowed Catholic prayers as prayers of surrender to Christ or expressions of an intention to dedicate their lives afresh to Christ can be appropriate. Thus, for example, as mentioned earlier, the prayer of St Ignatius Loyola can be used to great effect.

Such prayers can be recited in common, or can be more effectively spoken individually. Such prayers can be followed by a prayer of acceptance by the leader.

4. Another way to give formal expression to a response to evangelisation is to provide a formula of commitment or dedication to Christ. It could take the form of a question and answer process. Or it can be a prayer which the person reads out. Such a prayer formula would be most effective when said individually. Following the prayer it is useful to add a formula of acceptance or a blessing over the person. This final act can confirm what has taken place.

There are many ways in which a response to the experience of hearing the Gospel can find expression. The important thing is that there is some way in which a person can give their own personal response. Such a moment of response can be very significant because they have put into words what is in their hearts. They have given formal expression to their desire to follow Christ and life the Christian life.

v. The Gift of the Holy Spirit

In response to the question of how they could respond to his preaching, St Peter commented that if they were baptised they would receive the gift of the Holy Spirit. St Peter was assuring them that to accept the salvation achieved through the death and resurrection of Jesus meant that the power of God's Holy Spirit would come upon them in the same way in which the Spirit had manifested his presence to the Apostles. This claim proposes a very important aspect to Christianity.

To be a Christian is not only to believe in and follow Jesus Christ; it is not only to participate in the salvation achieved for us, but it is to receive the Holy Spirit as an active presence of God's ongoing saving work in our lives.

The New Testament gives clear testimony that the Christian was to benefit from the active presence of the Holy Spirit. Jesus spoke of the Spirit coming upon his disciples after his ascension.[85] St John comments on this a number of times in his Gospel. He says that in contrast to John the Baptists washing in the Jordan, Jesus would baptise with the Holy Spirit and fire. The Acts of the Apostles gives steady witness to the advent of the Spirit into the lives of those who are baptised.[86]

An essential part of the kerygma is to address the fact that coming to faith in Jesus Christ will lead to the advent of the Spirit in the Christian's life. This coming of the Spirit may, at times, be recognised by particular manifestations as the New Testament witnesses. Or it may be that the silent coming of the Spirit produces some discernible good fruits in the life of the believer.

Even if there is no discernible evidence of the Spirit the promise of Christ holds true. The Christian life is a life in the Spirit.

The proclamation of the kerygma should involve teaching on the gift and activity of the Holy Spirit. The presentation should encourage expectation that the Spirit will be an active agent in the Christian life. This teaching offers the opportunity to speak of what is a distinguishing characteristic of Christianity – that it is not just a philosophy or a morality but it is allowing the God of love to act in a decisive way within us and pour forth his Grace upon us.

The Christian lives a life in the Spirit. God is at work transforming

---

85 See John 14:15.
86 The Acts of the Apostles mentions five separate instances of the dramatic outpouring of the Holy Spirit on believers. They are 2:1-4, 4:28-31, 8:15-17, 10:44 and 19:6.

us. The Christian life is a life empowered by the Spirit so that we become truly "God's work of art" (Ephesians 2:10).

The New Testament gives eloquent testimony to the experience of the works of the Holy Spirit. St Peter experienced the tangible coming of the Holy Spirit on Cornelius and his household as he preached to them.[87] St Paul mentions various remarkable spiritual gifts obviously in evidence in the Christian community in Corinth following his preaching there. He speaks of preaching and teaching gifts, of gifts of prophesy and healing. He refers to the gift of Tongues[88] and to the gift of interpreting Tongues. These are by any account extraordinary spiritual gifts. In other places he provides other lists of gifts. For example in his Letter to the Romans (12:6-8) he speaks of prophesy, teaching, serving, exhortation, giving, leadership and compassion. In his Letter to the Ephesians (4:11) he defines certain roles in the community as being gifts of the Spirit. He specifically mentions the roles of apostle, prophet, evangelist, pastor/teacher.

The Christian life is not just a moral life but it is essentially a spiritual life. St Paul teaches that the Christian is one who is interested in the spiritual because "the Spirit of God has made his home in you" (Romans 8:9).

vi. Members of the Body of Christ

In considering the essential content of the Christian kerygma we have been referring to the first Christian proclamation given by St Peter at Pentecost. The Acts of the Apostles which records

---

87 See Acts chapter 10.
88 Sometimes called *glossalia*. This gift always follows the public exercise of the gift of tongues. In 1 Corinthians 14, St Paul required that all speech in Christian worship should be intelligible. This required that speech given in an unknown tongue be interpreted in the common language of the gathered Christians.

the event follows the account of the preaching by St Peter with a description of the first Christian community in Jerusalem. We can note a certain sequence here: preaching leads to conversion, conversion releases the Spirit, and those living the new life in the Spirit come together in community. Acts of the Apostles describes the first Christian community in these words, "The faithful all lived together and owned everything in common" (2:44). It identifies four elements present in the first Christian community. They were faithful to the teaching of the Apostles. They lived in a spirit of brotherhood. They celebrated the "breaking of the bread". And they prayed regularly together.

A final element in the presentation of the kerygma needs to be on the Church. It is clear that the Lord himself envisaged that the life of his disciples was to have a corporate dimension. The Christian life is not just a personal relationship with Jesus, but is called to be lived out within the Christian community.

From the beginning God planned that there would be a people who would be his very own. There is a refrain that runs through the Old Testament – I will be your God and you will be my people.[89] St Peter emphasised that the identity of being the People of God was passed to the Christians. In his first Letter St Peter says, "But you are a chosen people, a royal priesthood, a holy nation, a people belonging to God, that you may declare the praises of him who called you out of darkness into his wonderful light" (1 Peter 2:9).

The Christian is called to live discipleship of Jesus Christ within a Christian community, within the Church. The New Testament witnesses to the intention that Jesus intended that his mission in the world would be continued through the Church headed by St Peter

---

89 See Exodus 6:7; Leviticus 26:12; Jeremiah 7:23, 11.4, 30:22; Ezekiel 36:28, 37:12; Ruth 1:8; Joel 2:26-7; Hosea 4:6; Psalm 50:7; I Chronicles 11:2.

and founded on the twelve Apostles, representing the Twelve Tribes of Israel.

Participation in the life of the Church occurs via its sacramental life. Entry into the Church is through Baptism and the accompanying Sacrament of Confirmation. The fullness of participation is realised in the celebration of the Eucharist. The other Sacraments provide important moments of grace on the Christian journey through life.

Models of the kerygma

There are any number of formal presentations of the kerygma that can be used in the evangelisation process. Two well-known examples are the *Life in the Spirit Seminar* and the *Alpha Course*.

The *Life in the Spirit Seminar* was developed within the Catholic Charismatic Renewal and has been widely used for over 40 years. It is a proven programme . It usually consists in seven weekly sessions.

The topics covered are: God's love (God loves us with everlasting love); Salvation (God freed us from darkness and the power of Satan through Jesus Christ); New Life (God wants to give us a new life through the Holy Spirit); Receiving God's gifts (How to turn to the Lord in repentance and faith); Session devoted to prayer for the Holy Spirit; Growth (the role of prayer, study, service and community); and finally Transformation in Christ (moving forward in the Life in the Spirit and a new relationship with the Lord).

In this programme a typical session includes prayer, songs of praise, a talk on the session theme followed by small group discussion.

The *Alpha* programme was developed at the Holy Trinity Anglican Parish, Brompton, London in 1977. It was designed as a basic course in Christianity. The programme is organised as a series of 10 sessions given once a week. The series concludes with a day or weekend away.

Each session begins with a meal and a talk is then presented, usually a video of teaching given by it chief promoter, Nicky Gumbel. It is followed by discussion in small groups. Topics covered include: is there more to life than this?; Who is Jesus?; Why did Jesus die?; How can we have faith?; Why and how do I pray?; How and why should I read the bible?; How does God guide us?

The course has been run widely across the main Christian denominations and has engaged several million people across the globe. It has been actively promoted by many Catholic bishops and has been adapted to Catholic teaching.

Apart from these two well-known programmes of evangelisation there are many others that present the basic kerygma. It is now possible to find a basic presentation of the kerygma that is suited to a particular situation. Such programmes can be very useful as a follow-up to an evangelistic event or mission.

9

Fostering the Christian Life

Evangelisation is not an end in itself. Once a person has come to faith it is important that they are nurtured in the faith. When Christ gave the great commission to his Apostles at the time of his Ascension there were three key elements to it. The first was to preach, the second was to baptise and the third was "to teach them all that I have commanded you".[90] The RCIA, for instance, includes a period of Mystogogical Catechesis as an element in the process of entering the Church. The period of mystagogy lasts from Easter Sunday until the completion of the Easter season, 50 days later on Pentecost Sunday and completes the initiation process. Those who have just shared in the sacraments of initiation are called Neophytes and during this period of Easter joy they reflect on what they have just gone through and look to the future as to how they can now share in the mission of Christ who came to bring salvation and life to the whole world. This period of time reminds the whole church that life in Christ constantly calls us to grow and to look for new ways to live the life of grace, personally and together.

Evangelisation must be continued through catechesis. Outside of the various new movements in the church who see ongoing formation as vital, parishes can struggle to offer effective nurturing of those newly baptised.

There is the first and obvious need to assist people in entering

---

90 See *Matthew* 28: 19-20.

into the sacramental life of the Church by regular reception of the Sacraments of Holy Communion and Reconciliation. Further to this there is the need to assist the newly baptised to develop a strong personal prayer life. The reading of Sacred Scripture and learning more of the teaching of the Church enables a person to move towards a more mature faith.

For a person who returns to the Church and has had some basic formation in faith the question of the nurturing of their newly recovered faith is also important.

While parishes may offer limited scope for this formation, it is important that there be other agencies for this formation. A diocese may offer a variety of courses on the Catholic faith designed to provide formation. There are a range of resources available through the media that can assist those particularly wishing to deepen their knowledge and understanding of Catholicism.

It remains an important area for the overall task of the Church in the new evangelisation.

Catechesis

The Church uses the word "catechesis" to describe the process of nurturing the faith of those who are preparing for the celebration of the sacraments. Catechesis aims at enabling people not only to know about Christ, but to come into "communion", in "intimacy" with him.[91] The word, "catechesis" involves eliciting and nourishing the faith of the candidates in order to lead them to a deeper relationship with Jesus Christ. It is more than just the communication of knowledge. There is a difference between what is often termed

---

91 "The definitive aim of catechesis is to put people not only in touch, but also in communion, in intimacy, with Jesus Christ". *Catechesi Tradendae*, n. 5.

"religious education" and what is seen in the preparation of candidates for the sacraments as "catechesis".

A way of expressing the purpose of catechesis is presented in these words:

> The Christian faith is, above all, conversion to Jesus Christ, full and sincere adherence to his person and the decision to walk in his footsteps. Faith is a personal encounter with Jesus Christ making of oneself a disciple of him. This demands a permanent commitment to think like him, to judge like him and to live as he lived. In this way the believer unites himself to the community of disciples and appropriates the faith of the Church.[92]

Sacramental preparation is much more than the important task of imparting information about the sacrament, important as this is. It involves nourishing the faith of the candidates in their journey of faith so that they will be able to live the Christian life fully and be engaged in the sacramental life of the Church.

Faith is a personal relationship with Jesus Christ and it is only possible through the work of the Holy Spirit. It cannot be achieved by the exercise of intelligence or logic. Faith is a work of grace.[93] Grace is mediated through people. St Paul taught that faith comes through hearing (Rom 10:17). At the same time knowledge helps light the way to understanding and entering more deeply into faith. The Catholic Catechism says, "We do not believe in formulas, but in the realities they express, which faith allows us to touch."[94]

---

92 *General Directory on Catechesis*, n. 53.
93 "Grace" refers to the participation in the divine life. This is achieved through the indwelling presence of the Holy Spirit.
94 *Catechism of the Catholic Church*, n. 170.

Growth in Christian character

Apart from developing their spiritual life and increasing their knowledge of the Catholic faith, there is also the need to grow in Christian character.[95] With the pervasiveness of the media, it is a challenge for every believer to "put on the mind of Christ". The general ethos of the society does not favour the nourishing of a genuinely Christian character. It is something that must be developed through a serious effort.

When a person is asked about what is the distinctive character of a Christian the usual response is that love should characterise the life of a Christian. This, of course, is quite correct. We are immediately aware of the Great Commandment – love God and love others. In relation to this response we would probably add qualities like compassion, kindness and acceptance of others. We may add qualities like a concern for social justice. Again, this is a good and appropriate response.

As Christians we would naturally look to the example and teaching of Jesus whom we would consider as our model. We readily recognise that he reflected these qualities. However, we do need to identify many of the other qualities that should be present in the life and character of a Christian.

The beginnings of growing in Christian character is to have a sound Christian anthropology, that is, an understanding of the nature of the human person revealed through Sacred Scripture. Our Christian understanding of the nature of the human person is often quite at odds with the understanding adopted by the world around us, particularly influenced as it is by modern psychology and contemporary trends in thought.

---

95 See *Become What You Are – Growing in Christian Character*, Julian Porteous, Modotti Press, 2012.

The Christian has a clear and distinctive understanding of the nature of human life. This is revealed to us in the Scriptures and proven in human experience.

Our faith immediately opens to us the understanding that we have been created by an act of God. This means that we are not just random results of some sort of evolutionary process. It means we exist because God who is love has created the universe and each human being. Simply put we can say that love wants to give life, and this is what God has done. This may be elemental but it gives us an assurance that we – each one of us – are loved by God. It also suggests that our life has worth and meaning. The love which God has for us has been mediated through our parents and many personal experiences. We have tasted love.

The Book of Genesis declares that what God created was good. We are not junk! There is an essential value and goodness in each of us. We can see this. I know that I have value as a human being. This is why the Catholic Church has been so strong on the dignity of every human person. This is, for instance, why we oppose abortion – the child in the womb has a dignity and has a right to be born.

But there is another side to human existence. We know it well – the reality of evil, of sin, of suffering, of temptation. As Christians we understand this through the story of the Fall of Adam and Eve. We understand that God gave us free will which is an important element to our human dignity, but this freedom has been used to choose the path of evil. Temptation and sin are daily realities for each of us. Like St Paul we say that we want to do good, but we just seem to do what is the wrong thing. Like him we cry out, "who will save me from this body doomed to death".

Here the Christian teaching comes into its own. The Gospels

recount the coming of the Son of God in the man Jesus of Nazareth. In particular we understand that Jesus chose to offer his life to the Father on our behalf. He was the sacrifice that freed us from the punishment due our sin. When Jesus cried out from the cross: "Father forgive them for they know not what they do," he was appealing to his Father not just for his cruel executioners, but for each of us.

Jesus offered himself on our behalf and released the floodgates of mercy and forgiveness. It is interesting to note that the first thing Jesus did when he appeared to his disciples after his Resurrection was to say to them, "Receive the Holy Spirit whose sins you forgive they are forgiven." In other words, through the power of the Holy Spirit we can be forgiven of our sins and rise up to a new life.

The Christian life is a life of Grace, a life whereby the Holy Spirit is an active agent in our life. God bestows the Holy Spirit upon us and undertakes a process of transforming us. St Paul captures this reality in his words in Ephesians, "You are God's work of art."

This, brief as it is, is what we can call Christian anthropology. It is the Christian understanding of where we came from and where we are going. It is how we understand ourselves and our lives. It gives us a vital self-understanding.

Pursuing the virtuous life

So this is the basis for the Christian life. But still we want to know how we can grow in Christian character.

There are some simple building blocks upon which we can build our Christian character. It is to take a path of growing in virtue. To do this we firstly identify key virtues and then we rely on two key aspects. Firstly, we exercise our free will in that we desire to become such a person. We make a personal effort. Growth in virtue will only happen when we decide to seek virtue. The second element is that we rely not on ourselves to achieve these goals, but we rely upon the grace of God to assist us. You see, God wants each of us to grow to be more perfectly his sons and daughters. He wants to help, and he will.

On that basis then let's look at the building blocks. To present the following steps I want to say from the outset that these are my own thoughts. They are grounded solidly in the Catholic tradition, and they are counter-cultural.

Briefly they can be presented as follows:

i. Self-discipline

This is called in Church language "asceticism". If you want to swim at the London Olympics then no matter what natural skills you have you will have to train. Training means sacrifice. There are no shortcuts to holiness. What I say to myself is that the goal is worth it and I am willing to pay the price. So we develop some basic disciplines to my life.

ii. Humility

The foundational virtue I wish to propose to you is the virtue of humility. "God resists the proud and comes to help the lowly", the Scripture teaches. The bible is full of teaching about the indispensable need for humility. God can only work in us if we let him. If we are full of ourselves we will not give space to God. So a good starting point is to want to be humble, and willing to pay a little price to achieve it.

iii. Obedience

The next virtue I would like to propose is that of obedience. In the age of doing your own thing, this is an important challenge for many of us. Jesus said that he came not to do his own will, but the will of the One who sent him. We need to be able to say sincerely – as we do in the Our Father – "not my will be done, but yours". The Christian is willing to open his future to God. Thus, our prayer can be "Jesus, I entrust my life into your hands". It is a trust thing. It is a surrender of ourselves into the hands of God. This is not an easy thing to do. We all want to be our own master.

iv. Justice

One of the classical virtues is that of justice. The way we could speak of it today is developing personal integrity. The temptation today is to do what is necessary to get the right result. It is often tempting to forsake principle for pragmatism. People can consider their own interests as setting the criteria for their actions. Personal integrity lifts us to a new level. What price do we place on truth? The Christian will be one who is just.

v. Chastity

When I think of the next virtue I like to think of chastity as the "guardian of love". We all know that chastity is a much maligned virtue today. Many think it is impossible to preserve chaste relationships particularly in preparing for marriage. Pornography – particularly available on the internet – is a great scourge. A Christian chooses chastity as the way of protecting the beauty of sex and letting it be a "guardian of love". It sets the standard for my relationships. Chastity will show us the way to self-giving love. It is the best preparation for marriage.

vi. Love

With these virtues in place we can then turn to what we recognise as the definitive Christian virtue and the crown of the Christian life: love. Coming to genuinely self-giving love will mean that many other things are in place in our life. We all want to be loving, compassionate and kind people. We like to think this is the sort of person we are. The mature Christian will have love at the heart of all their actions. It will indeed become the crowning of a genuine Christian life. This love will be life-giving to others. Others will be the richer for having known us.

vii. Service

While love is the crowning of the Christian life, this love will flow into a life of service. The Christian is one who gives generously of themselves for the good of others. A mature Christian will be concerned about others and the society in which they live. They will work for the betterment of others. Their life will be other-directed. A mature Christian will be one who is involved. Christians do not hide in the shadows, but come out into the light. They are meant to be "salt of the earth and light of the world". Christians have always been at the forefront of helping those in need. This is the imperative of the desire to love.

viii. Hope and Joy

There is one final area of virtue that I think needs to be mentioned. Developing a mature Christian character will produce certain fruits in one's life. It will naturally (or better, supernaturally) result in a person being a person of hope and joy. By definition a Christian is a positive, hope-filled person. And Christians have a joy that radiates forth from them. This is not something that is put on or false. Christians have a light-heartedness. These are the signs of a genuinely Christian character.

A mature Christian is an attractive person, an inspiring person. This is what each of us can become.

Putting on Christ

The Christian lives by a deeply personal relationship with Jesus Christ. He, Christ, is the way, truth and life for them. Uniting our life with Christ and allowing the grace of salvation to flow in us, enables us to grow in Christian character. We will grow because we are allowing the principles of growth to be at work in us. The Christian life is a life whereby we are being transformed by the grace of God and becoming more and more in the image of Christ. St Paul speaks of "putting on Christ".[96]

To facilitate this, though, we need to identify those virtues that are the marks of a Christian and walk steadily in this path. We grow, as we have seen, by cooperating with divine grace.

---

96 See *Romans* 13:14.

10

Role of the Lay Person in the New Evangelisation

It is not without significance that when Pope John Paul first taught authoritatively about the new evangelisation it was in a document addressed to lay people. The document was entitled *Christifideles Laici*. It was published in 1988, ten years into his pontificate.

In other words, the Pope proposes that the task of the new evangelisation is not only the responsibility of priests and religious, but in a particular way is the task of the lay person living in the world. The Pope is calling on lay people to engage in what he sees as the great task of the Church in this time.

Pope John Paul noted in this document that there were new movements among the lay people emerging in the Church. These communities and groups often emerged from among lay people. Many have lay founders. These various movements have not only generated a renewed life among their members but have often engaged in forms of evangelisation. They have found new and innovative ways to express the Gospel message. These new initiatives are proving fruitful. The Pope encouraged these movements to confidently develop their new ways to evangelise in union with the Church.

It is one of the distinguishing features of the new evangelisation that it is a work of lay people who participate in the new movements that have sprung up in the Church over the past 50 years. While priests and religious work alongside them, the initiative often belongs to the lay people themselves.

Pope John Paul saw the significance of the ecclesial movements. He recognised the apostolic dynamism of the movements and saw them as a significant presence in the Church: "The great blossoming of these movements and the manifestations of energy and ecclesial vitality which characterise them are certainly to be considered one of the most precious fruits of the vast and profound spiritual renewal promoted by the last Council."

In 1998 he said that the movements "represent one of the most significant fruits of that springtime in the Church which was foretold by the Second Vatican Council". He went on to add that the movements have "a very precise – we can say irreplaceable – function in the Church". In his encyclical letter, *Redemptoris Missio* (1990), the Pope saw the movements as "a true gift of God both for the new evangelisation and for missionary activity properly so-called". He spoke of the movements as "a new Pentecost for the Church".

Key Church teaching[97]

In the 1980s the Church began serious dialogue with the movements as a whole. There had been dialogue with various individual movements in the past, particularly as founders began discussing with the Church their status within the structures of the Church, but by the 1980s the Church began to call the movements together and commence a deeper reflection on their identity and their place in the Church. An international meeting with ecclesial movements took place in Rome

---

[97] This and the following sections are taken from *A New Wine and Fresh Skins, Ecclesial movements in the Church*, Julian Porteous, Modotti Press, 2010.

in September 1981. A second meeting took place in March 1987. The third was 1998. In 1999 there was a follow-up meeting of bishops ("the ecclesial movements in the pastoral solicitude of bishops") in Speyer (Germany).

These meetings were significant in that they laid the foundations for magisterial statements which became vital indicators of the growing relationship between the Church and the movements. Movements became seen as a gift for the Church and the Church, in entering into dialogue with them, drew them to her heart. This was a process of great importance both for the movements themselves and for the Church. We will track some of the key outcomes of this process.

Key elements of papal statements[98]

We will identify some of the key elements of statements about the nature and significance of the new movements made by the magisterium, particularly in the person of the Pope.

I would like to mention five key elements.

i. The importance of ecclesial movements for the Church

Pope John Paul saw the significance of the ecclesial movements and spoke of them in more general terms in 1981. By 1987 he recognised the apostolic dynamism of the movements and saw them as a significant presence in the Church: "The great blossoming of these movements and the manifestations of energy and ecclesial vitality which characterise them are certainly to be considered one of the most precious fruits of the vast and profound spiritual renewal promoted by the last Council."[99]

---

98 I am following here the thought of Luis Navarro JCD, in his article, "New Ecclesial Movements and Charisms: Canonical Dimensions" produced in the *Philippine Canonical Forum*, IV (2002).

99 Address, 2 March 1987, n.1.

In 1998 he said that the movements "represent one of the most significant fruits of that springtime in the Church which was foretold by the Second Vatican Council".[100] He went on to add that the movements have "a very precise – we can say irreplaceable – function in the Church." In his encyclical letter, *Redemptoris Missio*, 1990, the Pope saw the movements as "a true gift of God both for the new evangelisation and for missionary activity properly so-called".[101] He spoke of the movements as "a new Pentecost for the Church".

ii. The role of charism

The source of a movement is a charism which is given to the founder. A charism is, as the word implies, a gift – a gift for the Church. Thus a charism is for the Church. The notion of charism which received special notice in the Constitution on the Church in Vatican II, is of vital significance when speaking of the movements. It proposes that movements are not merely human undertakings, but have a divine source, an inspiration, which is usually incarnated in the spiritual vision of the founder.

Pope John Paul often referred to the complementary role of charism and institution. He saw them as "mutually complementary". In his 1987 address to the movements he said:

> In the Church, both the institutional and the charismatic aspects, both the hierarchy and association and movements of the faithful, are co-essential and share in fostering life, renewal and sanctification, though in different ways.[102]

iii. Movements form around a charism

Movements become a reality when groups of the faithful respond to a charism. The power of the charism so engages them that they

---

100 Message, 27 May 1998, n. 2.
101 *Redemptoris Missio*, n. 72.
102 Address, 2 March 1987, n. 3.

associate in order to live the charism. Pope John Paul addressed this phenomenon in these words:

> In the Church's history we have continually witnessed the phenomenon of more or less vast groups of the faithful, which, under a mysterious impulse of the Spirit, have been spontaneously moved to join together in pursuit of certain charitable or sanctifying ends. This has come about in relation to the particular needs of the Church in their day, and even involved collaboration in the Church's essential and permanent mission.[103]

What is important is that the forming of a movement is somehow a fruit of the impulse of the Spirit, with the free will of those who embrace the life of the movement. It is also important to recognise that the founder, embodying the charism, has a special influence. Again, as the Pope expresses it, "The passage from the original charism to the movement happens through the mysterious attraction that the founder holds for all those who become involved in his spiritual experiences."[104]

iv. An outworking of the grace of baptism

The ground upon which people from all states of life in the Church can become involved in an ecclesial movement is their common baptism. Indeed, we can say that the movements are simply the actualisation of baptismal grace. Pope John Paul commented on this when he said, "Even in the diversity of their forms, these movements are marked by a common awareness of the 'newness' which baptismal grace brings to life, through a remarkable longing to reflect on the mystery of communion with Christ and with their brethren."[105]

---

103 Address, 2 March 1987, n. 2.
104 Address, 30 May 1998, n. 6.
105 Message, 27 May 1998, n. 2.

Members of movements in effect live out the full reality of their Christian identity and calling. Again we refer to the words of the Pope, "members of the Church who find themselves in associations and movements seek to live, under the impulse of the Spirit, the Word of God in their concrete lives".[106] He commented that the movements "have helped you all to rediscover your baptismal vocation".[107]

What is significant about participation in the movements is that the Christian life of the members is not just partially involved, but their whole Christian life is engaged. Movements are more than associations where individuals contribute to a work or cause in the Church, they are rather a completely involving experience.

v. **Communion with the Church**

Movements can be composed of Catholics and have a Catholic identity but there is a danger that they can operate outside the structures of the Church. Sometimes they can be elitist or be critical of the "ordinary" life of the Church. This can be a temptation at the beginning in the first flush of enthusiasm and discovery of their charism and life. Pope John Paul recognised this and particularly at the 1998 gathering of communities called for a new level of maturity by which the movements could come to a better sense of their place in the Church. He said, "Today a new stage is unfolding before you: that of ecclesial maturity ... the Church expects from you the 'mature' fruits of communion and commitments."[108]

At a meeting with bishops one year later he said:

> This journey requires of movements an ever stronger communion with the Pastors God has chosen and

---

106 Address, 2 March 1987, n. 3.
107 Address, 30 May 1998, n. 7.
108 Address 30 May 1998, n. 6.

consecrated to gather and sanctify his people in the light of faith, hope and charity, because 'no charism dispenses a person from reference and submission to the Pastor of the Church'.[109]

The teaching in *Christifideles Laici*

It was shortly after the international meeting with the ecclesial movements that the Pope presided over the 1987 Synod of Bishops on the theme of the role of the lay person in the Church and in the world. No doubt the experience with the movements influenced the Pope's contribution to this synod. His interventions were connected specifically with the role of movements in the Church. In particular his post synodal apostolic exhortation, *Christifideles Laici*, explored the "ecclesial criteria" for movements. He provided a set of expectations as to how movements can be soundly in and with the Church. He listed five key criteria ("Criteria of Ecclesiality")[110]:

- The primacy given to the call to holiness – the pope recognised that movements must be instrumental in leading its members to holiness. There must be "a more intimate unity between the everyday life of its members and their faith".

- A responsibility for professing the faith – here the Pope saw that authentic movements do not just teach the faith but enable their members to profess the faith.

- A witness to a strong and authentic filial communion with the Pope. The Pope is "the visible principle and foundation of unity".

---

109 Message, 18 June 1999, The Pope quoted from *Christifideles Laici*, n. 24.
110 *Christifideles Laici*, n. 30.

- Conformity to and participation in the Church's apostolic goals. The movements are to be united with the missionary spirit of the Church.

- A commitment to a presence in human society. The Pope here is conscious that the movements need to have an awareness of contributing to the strengthening of human culture.

He concludes this consideration of the "Criteria of Ecclesiality" by saying:

> The fundamental criteria mentioned at this time find their verification in the *actual fruits* that various group forms show in their organisational life and the works they perform, such as: the renewed appreciation for prayer, contemplation, liturgical and sacramental life, the reawakening of vocations to Christian marriage, the ministerial priesthood and the consecrated life; a readiness to participate in programmes and Church activities at the local, national and international levels; a commitment to catechesis and a capacity for teaching and forming Christians; a desire to be present as Christians in various settings of social life and the creation and awakening of charitable, cultural and spiritual works; the spirit of detachment and evangelical poverty leading to a greater generosity in charity towards all; conversion to the Christian life or the return to Church communion of those baptised members who have fallen away from the faith.[111]

It is clear from this that the Pope has high expectations of what the movements can contribute to the Church.

---

111 *Christifideles Laici*, n. 30.

The witness to a new life

The most powerful influence of the movements is their witness to a new vitality in Christian life. Pope Paul stated in *Evangelii Nuntiandi*:

> For the Church, the first means of evangelisation is the witness of an authentically Christian life, given over to God in a communion that nothing should destroy and at the same time given to one's neighbour with limitless zeal. As we said recently to a group of lay people, "Modern man listens more willingly to witnesses than to teachers, and if he does listen to teachers, it is because they are witnesses." ... It is therefore primarily by her conduct and by her life that the Church will evangelise the world, in other words, by her living witness of fidelity to the Lord Jesus – the witness of poverty and detachment, of freedom in the face of the powers of this world, in short, the witness of sanctity.[112]

Many of those involved in the various movements comment on the fact that encountering the movement has resulted in a profound change to their faith and way of living their Christian life. Many of the movements are instruments of conversion. Mass-going Catholics will testify to a new-found understanding of what it means to be a Catholic. Their lives have taken on a new shape – their interior spiritual life is now so much stronger. Family life is more seriously Catholic. Their attitudes to the world have changed from a degree of accommodation to that of being counter-cultural. They have a clearer moral understanding and grasp the teaching of the Church with a renewed vigour.

Those in the movements have found not just a fullness of truth about the Christian life, but they have found joy and peace. They

---

112 *Evangelii Nuntiandi*, n. 41.

are enthusiastic about their Catholic faith and long to share this new awareness with others.

It is not unusual for family, friends and acquaintances to notice a difference in them in the early stages of becoming involved in the life of one of the movements. These early phases of discovery of the Christian life often provide precious opportunities for the person to give witness to what has happened to them. They often do so in the first bloom of their new way of living as a Christian. This witness carries a particular efficacy.

One of the common forms of evangelisation by the movements is the use of testimony or witness. A person is invited to share their own personal experience of coming into the charism of the movement and how it has altered their life. Some will witness to a radical change from a life far from God to a new life in the Spirit. Others will testify to the ways in which the movement has led them to deeper faith.

The Charismatic based movements often use testimony. A person will give witness to the experience of conversion or the outpouring of the grace of the Holy Spirit, or perhaps a healing that has taken place. The value of such witness is that it is from a person's own life. It has a validity in that it is something real for the person. The hearer is free to accept it or not. Often such a witness carries with it the humility and gratitude of the person for what God has done.

The Neo Catechumenal Way has the bold programme of sending Itinerant Catechists to very challenging pastoral situations, like Eastern Europe, Muslim countries and China. These families firstly provide a witness to the Christian life by the example of their family life. When they arrive in an area which has little or no presence of the structures of the Church and the local inhabitants have no exposure to the Catholic faith, then witness becomes the first and primary source for evangelisation. The witness of Christian love and the quality of Christian family life can be an evangelising moment, even before any explicit proclamation takes place.

Conclusion: the beauty of being a Christian

The second gathering of the new movements and communities in 2006 came together under the theme of "The beauty of being a Christian." This theme reveals an aspect of what the new movements have brought to the Church. They have helped their members to rediscover the beauty of being a Christian, and the members of the new movements can give a witness to the world of the beauty of being a Christian.

Pope Benedict addressed this theme at his homily to the gathered members of the new movements in St Peter's Square at the Vigil of Pentecost:

> Dear friends, we want to be these children of God for whom creation is waiting, and we can become them because the Lord has made us such in Baptism. Yes, creation and history – they are waiting for us, for men and women who are truly children of God and behave as such. Time and again in history the advent of the Holy Spirit has brought the experience of the beauty of being a Christian to those swept up in the moments of Grace – the monks in deserts, the monks living under the Rule of St Benedict, those inspired by the ideals of St Francis of Assisi, those seeking to live the Imitation of Christ, the students of Paris reaching out to the poor, and now those called to a new way of holiness in the movements in the Church.[113]

---

113 Pope Benedict XVI, Address to new movements, 3 June 2006.

The new ecclesial movements show a strong orientation towards apostolic activity. In particular they have embraced the new evangelisation promoted by Pope John Paul. Evangelisation involves explicit proclamation of the Gospel message, but words can be cheap. The new ecclesial movements are able to be effective in evangelisation because they can witness to what they proclaim by the quality of their Christian life. These movements reveal an expression of Christian life in their corporate existence, but more importantly it is in the example given by individual members of the movement that offers a witness.

Evangelisation needs to be accompanied by a witness of life. The power of testimony to the Catholic faith is to be found when it is a visible lived reality. The movements witness to a new way of life. Before examining evangelisation we will comment on the importance of witness.

11

Methods of Evangelisation

We will now turn our attention to the "how" of evangelisation. To do this we will explore some of the arenas in which evangelisation can take place. The response to the call to a new evangelisation has already taken many surprising and effective forms within the Church. The ways of evangelisation must always work to be responsive to the circumstances of people and cultures. Thus the means by which we evangelise never stay the same. What was effective once may not be effective at another time or in another location. While the message we proclaim does not change in essence, the ways in which we go about proclaiming the message are constantly changing.

An evangelist must understand the times and the mentality of people. An evangelist must be able to couch the message so that it penetrates the reality of people's lives. Pope Paul comments in *Evangelii Nuntiandi*:

> The obvious importance of the content of evangelisation must not overshadow the importance of the ways and means. This question of "how to evangelise" is permanently relevant, because the methods of evangelising vary according to the different circumstances of time, place and culture, and because they thereby present a certain challenge to our capacity for discovery and adaptation.

The new evangelisation does require a capacity for initiative grounded in an instinct for the inner needs of people. It requires a certain immersion into the culture so that the message can relate to the actual experience of people. An evangelist to be effective will listen to the culture, note the shifts in attitudes and be able to "hear" the inner cry of the human heart.

In responding to his call to engage in evangelisation, Pope Paul urged the Church to assume the responsibility "for reshaping with boldness and wisdom, but in complete fidelity to the content of evangelisation, the means that are most suitable and effective for communicating the Gospel message to the men and women of our times".[114]

This remains both a challenge and an exciting possibility. Like St Paul we must be all things to all people.[115] We must enter the culture in order to redeem the culture.

Bold innovation

Pope Paul spoke of "reshaping with boldness and wisdom" the means by which we are to evangelise. Evangelisation today calls for creativity and innovation. Part of this new boldness is finding new ways in which to penetrate a growing secular environment with the beauty and inspiration that the Gospel offers. It is to shake off false images of what Christianity is about. It is to show how faith in Jesus Christ brings about a transformation of human life.

This boldness and creativity is born of the experience of living one's faith in a rich and rewarding way. Those who are alive in faith

---

114 *Evangelii Nuntiandi*, n. 40.
115 See I Corinthians 9:19-23. St Paul comments that he is prepared to adapt himself to whatever group of people he engages with in order that he may evangelise them. He says, "I have become all things to all people so that by all possible means I might save some. I do all this for the sake of the Gospel that I may share in its blessings."

and have a deep appreciation of what faith means to them will be best equipped to be advocates of the Christian life.

One of the very exciting aspects of the Church today is that new and inventive ways in which the Gospel message can be presented are being utilised. We are witnessing a Catholic resurgence as the Gospel is being communicated in today's world.

Let us consider some of these new ways in which we can evangelise.

Personal witness

As we mentioned at the conclusion of the previous chapter, personal witness is of prime importance in evangelisation. Words are not enough by themselves. People today look to see what effect the Christian faith has on the way a person lives. Pope Paul stated, "Modern man listens more willingly to witnesses than to teachers, and if he does listen to teachers, it is because they are witnesses."[116] If the Christian is no different from those around them then the Christian message will be deemed to have little to offer. This is a challenge to all who are involved in evangelisation. People need to see in the evangeliser something different which is attractive and inspiring. The evangelising task of the Church will need saints to carry forth its work.

Every believer in the normal course of life has many opportunities to show that their life is shaped by their faith. Opportunities often emerge whereby we can share our faith or explain our beliefs. Such a sharing of our faith does not need to be deeply theological, but can simply be an expression of our faith as we understand it. Often people of no faith are fascinated by someone who has something to live by and has beliefs that underpin their lives. We should not be

---

116 *Evangelii Nuntiandi*, n. 24.

embarrassed about "giving an account of the hope that lies within us" (See I Peter 3:15). What to us may seem normal can be something which fascinates and attracts those who have no clear moral or spiritual foundation to their life.

In the area of personal witness it is very helpful if a believer has reflected upon their own journey of faith and so can, if asked, give a simple testimony to how God has touched their life or shaped the pattern of their life. A testimony does not need to be a story of dramatic conversion. It can be simply an account of how one has sensed the presence of God. It may take the form of a simple explanation of what faith means to them.

What attracts people is not an array of arguments and explanations but the example of someone who is at peace, joyful and open in love to others. While there is a place for apologetics and theological argument, basic evangelisation most often begins by an interpersonal interaction where there is a sharing of the blessing that faith has brought to the living of life.

The power of testimony

To be an evangelist the starting point can be the preparation of a personal testimony. It may be two minutes or ten minutes in length. A testimony is always a simple and humble sharing. It is not teaching nor in any way an effort to convince by argument. A testimony will seek to give the honour to God and is not self-glorification. It is an account of what God has done or what faith has meant. It is expressed with a spirit of humble gratitude to God. It is shared in a spirit of love and openness to the other.

Sharing a personal testimony is a powerful way to make Christ present to others. He becomes more than an historical figure. Instead, he is alive and active in the life of someone the listener knows.

Today's culture values experiences very highly. So we cannot underestimate the power of a personal testimony. Another advantage of a personal testimony is that it doesn't require refutation. It is not a hypothesis being posed. Instead it invites the listener to hear a sharing of personal experience. It puts no demand on the listener.

In giving one's testimony is it important to know how long to speak. One guide is that of the traffic lights – red, yellow, green. If the person is not ready to hear what we say then we should remain silent rather than seem pushy or a bore (the red light). If the person seems open but is tuning out (yellow light) we should not persist. If the person is genuinely curious and willing to listen (green light) we can continue. It is simply a matter of being alert to the signs. It is counterproductive to press on when the listener is not open to receive what we offer.

Sometimes a person may ask a question about the Catholic faith. If there is a genuine curiosity then there is the opportunity to offer an expression of one's faith. Rather than attempt a theological explanation it is often wiser to simply explain one's own understanding, particularly focusing on how a particular belief is helpful.

To share our testimony well takes prayerful preparation so that we can have "ready answer"[117] to offer those who listen to us. It would be good to take our faith story to prayer and ask the Holy Spirit to show us the important markers or points of decision that will be helpful to others in their faith.

A testimony usually has a simple structure consisting of a before, a key experience, and an after. Reflecting on our lives we can see that a change has occurred in us. It may been a gradual process. Nevertheless, we can see that there has been a change. This is what we can share.

---

117 See I Peter 3:15.

When considering the "before" of the testimony there are some questions that may help:

- What things were most important to you?
- What did your life revolve around?
- Why were they so important?
- What basic need were you trying to fulfil?
- How did you try to satisfy that need?

When considering the key experience of your testimony these questions may help:

- When did you first hear the message of Christ?
- What was your reaction?
- Was it an event or series of events that brought you to the point of decision?
- Was it a friend/family member who encouraged you?
- Why did you make the decision to follow/trust Jesus?
- How did you specifically do that?

Talking about the time after the experience is crucial. This is what gives people an understanding of what it means to be a follower of Christ. It is important to be realistic here and not to paint a picture of "happily ever after". Life still holds challenges for the followers of Christ but there is grace available to help us. This is what we need to communicate. The following questions may help in considering the 'after':

- How did Christ specifically begin to satisfy the basic need you had before?
- What changes have occurred in your life as a result?
- How do you know Christ is in your life?

Once we have prayed through this we can ask some good Catholic friends to listen to your testimony. They can give their reactions and offer advice of how to improve the testimony. What spoke to them? What did they want to know more about? Was there anything that didn't seem relevant?

In sharing our testimony the following principles can be helpful:

- Keep it true – avoid being overly dramatic.
- Keep it real – avoid "church" jargon.
- Keep it simple – strive to give glory to God not to impress the hearer.
- Keep it personal – like a one-to-one conversation (use "I", "me" or "my" rather than "you").

Once we have our testimony prepared and clear in our minds we can look for opportunities to share our testimony with others. The people we share with are most likely going to be people who know and trust us. If you think that a conversation may be lending itself to sharing our testimony, say something like this, "I have found something that really helped me ... May I share it with you?" Once we have shared our testimony, be prepared, if the listener has been visibly moved, to back it up by offering to say a simple prayer with them or by inviting them to some event where they can go deeper in their faith.

Public witness to faith

Public witness to our faith is important as life around us is dominated by secular images. Public religious events help people be aware of the presence of men and women of faith in their midst.

One effective form of public witness which has been a significant part of Catholic tradition is that of the religious procession. In times past when many European societies were Christian, processions were a normal part of the culture. In the 13th century for instance, a procession of the Blessed Sacrament through the streets of the town on the feast of Corpus Christi developed an expression of the devotion of the people in the Real Presence.[118] It was a major event in the town's calendar. The whole town turned out and much preparation went into the procession. It was a public expression of the faith of the people. Today we see in many countries religious processions to celebrate particular feasts significant to that culture.

In recent years in many Western countries, processions have fallen into decline. Some have felt that they belong to an earlier "medieval" mentality and are out of place in a more "sophisticated" Catholicism. However we are witnessing a resurgence of interest in such processions. While such practices are expressions of Catholic faith and devotion, when taken into secular contexts they can be evangelising opportunities.

These days a procession through the streets of the secular city can be a novelty to many people but at the same time something which seizes their interest. Many stop to observe the event curious as to its meaning. A Catholic procession complete with incense, candles, vestments and of course – if it is a Eucharistic procession – the monstrance carried under a canopy, is a colourful event. It gives expression to devotion to spiritual realities and the reverence of those in the procession has an impact on the passer-by.

---

118 Processions have long had a place in Catholic practice. The Liturgy proposes a number of processions. For example the procession with candles at Candlemas (2 February), the procession with palms on Palm Sunday as well as processions with statues of various Saints on their special feasts. There is the taking of the Sacrament to the Altar of Repose after the Mass on Holy Thursday. The Procession of the Blessed Sacrament on the Feast of Corpus Christi is another expression of this tradition.

Many who have never been inside a church to witness Catholic liturgy and prayer are exposed to our traditions when a procession is held on the streets. It is a witness to our faith in transcendental realities. It is a simple and yet strong testimony to faith.

It is possible to hold processions of various kinds. A Marian procession with a statue of the Blessed Virgin in conjunction with a Marian feast can be easily organised by a parish community, for instance. The Stations of the Cross on Good Friday morning can be conducted through the streets of a suburb or town.

The Christian custom of Christmas Carols has been taken over in many instances now by groups that see them as attractive events for Christmas. Where possible Catholic parishes could reclaim them as genuinely Christian celebrations. Carols held in public locations are very appealing to families, particularly those with young children. There is the opportunity for evangelisation of families.

As the world in which many people live today has no expressions of Christianity, taking to the streets in public witness can draw people who have little contact with faith or the Church to understand the religious significance of major Christian celebrations like Christmas or Easter or major feasts.

It can be very useful to have people who fulfil an evangelising role by accompanying the procession and are ready to explain the event, answer questions, hand out literature or devotional items related to the procession and perhaps even share their testimony to people along the way.

The World Youth Day gives a very clear expression to this. Its key events are held in public locations. The Stations of the Cross are held in the streets of the city. The final Mass is proceeded by a pilgrimage through the streets. In every city where the World Youth Day has been held it has had a remarkable impact on the local citizens. They are exposed to young people in their hundreds of thousands full of joy and love. The young people themselves become the most powerful witness to what the Christian life offers.

The World Youth Day event gives powerful testimony of the youth and vibrancy of the Church. It shatters impressions that the Church is old and dying. It reveals that the Christian life is attractive to the young.

Street evangelisation

There is a temptation among Catholics to see faith as something private – between me and God. Indeed we are often told by our society not to impose our views on others. One bold response to this is street evangelisation.

There is a need in our growing secular environments to be out there among the people – to be "in the market place". At the World Youth Day in 1993, Pope John Paul said: "Do not be afraid to go out onto the streets and into public places as the first Apostles did, to preach Christ and the good news of salvation in the squares of cities, towns and villages. This is no time to be ashamed of the Gospel."[119] The Pope makes it clear that the Church cannot just call people to its own environment, but must reach out and engage with people in their situations of everyday life. The Church needs to be seen as present in the marketplace.

Many groups involved in evangelisation have seen the value of street evangelisation. Often people are surprised to discover Catholics being engaged in such activities. We take our example from Christ himself who, while he speaking in the synagogues and in the temple

---
119 Pope John Paul II, World Youth Day homily, 15 August 1993, Denver.

precincts, spent most of his time among the people in their towns and countryside. The Church of our time needs to take its message to the streets in humility and joy.

It is important that when we are involved in street evangelisation that we clearly identify ourselves as Catholics. We can do this by having a typical Catholic image like the Sacred Heart or an image of the Virgin Mary. People are often surprised to discover that Catholics would evangelise on the streets. While the Church is often the target for negative criticism and "Catholic bashing" has become endemic in much of the media, the fact is that there are many who are drawn to what the Catholic Church has to offer. They know that the Church stands for something. They may secretly admire what the Church teaches and does. Being seen as Catholic helps people in responding to our overtures to them.

Street evangelisation can take many different forms. It can consist in a group singing on the streets and those who gather to listen are engaged in conversation. Music is attractive when done well – a schola singing Gregorian chant can be particularly attractive. Short dramas can also be an effective way of engaging people.

Some shopping centres will allow a Catholic information table to be set up. A simple banner identifying the group can be enough to attract people to come and examine what is on offer. Conversations can lead to people going away with some Catholic literature or a holy object.

The key in street evangelisation is to find opportunities to engage people in conversation. One simple way is to stand at a bus stop. We need to speak to people when they have time to listen. Striking up a conversation at a natural level can easily move to a religious theme. One can ask after some initial pleasantries, for instance, if the listener is a Catholic or believes in God. If the conversation begins simply people can be happy to share their attitudes to such basic issues. Again, the use of the traffic lights guide can be helpful here.

When engaged in street evangelisation it is important to have a number of resources available to give to listeners. For example one can have a Miraculous Medal, or a set of rosary beads, a holy card, or prayer card, a New Testament, or even the *Compendium of the Catechism*. As the conversation concludes it is important that the person walks away with something as a reminder of the conversation.

Street evangelisation often does not produce immediate fruits. However, it is an important public witness to the existence and apostolic zeal of the Church. Now, in many secularised cities, it would appear that Christianity is silent and invisible. Apart from the existence of Church buildings there is little public presence of the Church. For many, Christianity is considered as dying or something that only attracts the elderly. The experience of meeting Catholics who are young (as many who engage in street evangelisation are) and alive in their faith, acts as an important witness to the fact that the Church is still very much alive and active.

It is also true that the action of being involved in street evangelisation strengthens the faith of the evangelisers. They are in the public arena declaring themselves as believers. Many people who may initially be uncomfortable with the idea find that, once they have done some street evangelisation, enjoy the experience. It builds up their faith and their confidence of sharing their faith.

Door-to-door visitation

Another expression of street evangelisation is going door-to-door in visitation. It is wise that evangelisers go in pairs: one talks and the other prays. It is useful if the visiting is linked to some event like a mission so that the evangelisers can invite the person they meet to some activity. It also gives a natural reason for the visit and the subject of conversation.

There are some practical tips in relation to door-to-door visitation. It is wise to visit in pairs with one man and one woman being best. It is good to establish a time devoted to the visitation – a couple of hours is best. It is important to present well, to be clean and tidy. One should always get permission from the parish priest and have parish information to offer or leave under the door. Take a notebook and pen to make notes about visits or contacts. Have a map of the parish streets and boundary of the parish. Keeping records and making revisits are crucial. It is important to wear parish name tags (first name is sufficient). Carry devotional items and literature that encourage and inspire which can be given to those who want them.

Many are daunted about what to do and say when the door opens. It is good to commence the visitation time with a prayer and to conclude the visitation time with a prayer. A good attitude to adopt is that we go as beggars in humility. We should exclude no-one and never judge a door, a person or a situation. Obey all signs on doors/letter boxes. Do not take unnecessary risks. Remember names and listen intently to what people may say. Accept hospitality if it is offered. Offer to pray for those in need, now and later. Do not put time limits on any particular visit. Use humour and lightheartedness to avoid arguments. We seek to offer the faith and not to impose it. If someone has been hurt by the Church or is hostile to it then listen in compassion and apologise for past hurts. It is important to know when to let things go and move on. In these conversations we simply give witness to our faith and leave the conversions to God.[120]

---

120 Adapted from "Evangelisation: Home visitation and street contacts" written by Josef Holzschuh PhD, based on the writings of Frank Duff.

Evangelising marriage and family

As we noted earlier, marriage and family are under particular pressure today. There is a need to develop an evangelisation strategy directed to married couples to assist them in developing genuinely Christian marriages and in creating a Christian home which is conducive to the nurturing of children in the Christian faith.

The starting point for this is the pre-marriage formation. It is an excellent opportunity to present the Christian vision of marriage. Pre-marriage formation is now an accepted part of preparation for marriage in the Church. The formation should seek to nurture the faith of the engaged couple and help them discover God's plan for married life.

Offering opportunities for married couples to be renewed in their marriage is an important service for couples today. A series of talks or a weekend can draw a couple into a deeper appreciation of the grace of the Sacrament of Matrimony. Couples seeking to enrich their marriage can be led into a deeper relationship with God. Building a Christian environment in the home is an important means of nurturing children in the Christian way of life.

In recent times the development of various men's movements has been a valuable means by which men are strengthened in their role as husbands and fathers. Such movements help to form men to take spiritual responsibility in the home.

The pro-life movement is an important evangelising instrument today. Its message about the sacredness of human life stands in stark contrast to the commonly held views of society. When the movement engages not so much on the political level but on the level of prayer and silent vigil in front of abortion clinics, it can have the capacity to change hearts. The struggle for a culture of life is a struggle conducted at the spiritual level. Law will not change until hearts change. The pro-life movement reflected in campaigns like 40 Days for Life has the capacity to be a powerful evangelising instrument.

Evangelisation programmes

There are various evangelisation programmes that have been developed in recent times. We spoke before of the Life in the Spirit Seminar and Alpha. They are good examples of programmes designed to meet the needs of people today. There are many more. When there is a desire to evangelise the means to do so will be found. Many evangelisation programmes have been developed to meet particular needs, for example, for teenage youth, for young married couples, for business people, for men. Often they emerge from an individual or group seeking to reach out to a particular group of people within their own social and cultural setting.

As we discussed before what is important is that such programmes move to the very heart of the Christian message. Evangelisation programmes cannot be presentations *about* the faith, but be effective means by which a person is engaged *with* the Gospel message. Every programme can be examined to see whether it is able to effectively lead someone to Christ. This must be the ultimate goal.

It is not enough, as St James, says just to look in the mirror and walk away.[121] A person needs to have the opportunity to put into action what has touched them. Faith is not just a feeling but a decision.

University apostolate

One very important area of evangelisation is the university campus. The history of the Church reveals how an effective presence of

---

121 See James 1:19-27.

the Church in universities can yield abundant fruit. So many saints were born through an adult discovery of the faith while undertaking tertiary study. An example is St Francis Xavier who was evangelised by his fellow student at the Sorbonne, St Ignatius Loyola.

The Church has many of its own universities and colleges across the world. These Catholic institutions provide great opportunities for evangelisation. Developing the clear Catholic identity of the institution is most important. A Catholic university must be Catholic not just in name but in fact.

Where the Church runs university colleges these colleges should have a healthy culture fostered by Christian beliefs and focused towards the formation of students in order to assist them to fulfil their flourishing as men and women of faith. The fully integrated nature of university colleges it a very powerful tool for evangelisation if as an institution they have these goals at their core.

The university years are important formative years. They are years in which many young people shape their belief systems and moral attitudes. University is a special time in a young adult's life as it opens up the wonder of new knowledge and new ideas. For many people it is a self-defining time where key life decisions are made.

The Church needs to be actively present during this process of formation. It needs to be able to present its perspective on the great issues of the day. University evangelisation offers opportunity to present the Catholic faith in an attractive way and offer students avenues to explore what the Catholic Church has to offer. Many university graduates go on to take important roles of leadership in their professions and in the society. Thus forming them in their faith and in a clear Catholic moral vision will enable their future roles of leadership to reflect Christian truth and moral outlook.

Evangelisation on university campus should be built around four pillars.

The first pillar concerns the intellectual level. Universities are places of ideas. Catholic campus ministry should offer formation on aspects of Catholic faith. The Church has a strong tradition of rigorous thought and has many positions on matters of faith and morals that are strikingly different from much of contemporary thought. In the face of the relativism which is so prevalent today the Church can offer clear moral teaching based on solid premises. In the face of secular humanism the Church can present a transcendental view of human life which brings about a more profound understanding of the nature of human life. Whether it be through guest speakers or series of talks on pertinent topics, Catholic campus ministry can present clear teaching which engages young people exploring the world of ideas.

A second pillar is the spiritual ministry. Campus ministry should offer the opportunity for daily Mass. It can offer opportunities for prayer in various forms. Through Scripture study groups it can help young Catholics to grow in knowledge of the Scriptures and to hear the Word of God for their lives. In direct evangelisation activities the campus ministry should concentrate on assisting young people at university to encounter Jesus Christ.

A third pillar for Catholic campus ministry is offering a community experience for young people. Many young tertiary students are away from their families and familiar settings. They need opportunities for social life. A Catholic society can offer much human support grounded in a spirit of faith and love. This area of service by the campus ministry opens up the possibility for peer-to-peer evangelisation where those more mature in faith can nurture those just beginning to discover or re-discover their Catholic faith. A healthy social scene can be offered that assists students in making choices which do not lead to morally and physically destructive situations, all too common in the broader university and young adult scene. A healthy social scene also allows students to possibly meet future spouses and participate in dating and courtship that is supported by a faith-filled culture.

The fourth pillar is the dimension of mission. Young people are often inspired to be engaged in works of compassion and service. Catholic campus ministry can offer mission opportunities within the city or organise mission trips during semester breaks.

The university years are key formational years for young people. The presence of the Church through an active campus ministry can produce much fruit.

Parish missions

Parish missions have been a significant part of Catholic life, especially since religious Congregations like the Vincentians and Redemptorists made missions a key component of their service to the Church.

The advent of the new evangelisation has opened up the possibility of developing missions which are shaped by the principles of the new evangelisation. Thus the preaching is more directly evangelical. Mission activities are "in the marketplace" as well as in the church. Such parish missions can be the work of priests and lay people working together.

Marketplace missionary activities can include:

- Talks in alternative venues, like pubs or cafés, which may attract people unwilling to enter a church.
- Letter box drops as a way of communicating to the people of an area.
- Door-to-door visitations to provide personal contact with people.

- House blessings as a way of engaging with families.
- Parish coffee stall on the street as a way of engaging with passers-by.
- Stalls in local shopping centers show the church as present and active.
- Street evangelisation through music or drama to attract the interest of people.
- Missionary visits to local schools, both Catholic and State, offering presentations to the students.
- A procession through local streets as a testimony to Catholic spirituality.
- Inviting locals to come into the church to light a candle and say a prayer can attract people to go inside a church.

Mission teams for youth

One of the fruits of the new movements emerging in the Church are the forming of youth mission teams. These teams are made up of young people, who after a short period of intensive training, volunteer for one year of evangelical service. The teams often travel together and live an intense experience of Christian life together. The National Evangelisation Teams which began in the United States is one example of such teams.

The power of music

The Catholic Church has a rich patrimony of music. The liturgy of the Church has inspired some of the most beautiful compositions in Western culture. These works, involving chant or polyphony accompanied by orchestra or organ are some of the finest expressions of the human spirit and they have been inspired by the Catholic faith.

One thinks of the sublime works of Bach, the Mozart Masses and the many stirring Requiems.

Similarly there is a vast repertoire of popular hymns that continue to be appreciated and sung down many centuries. One only has to think of Christmas carols which are sung every year and universally loved.

Music is a vital medium to give expression to the faith. Music is a powerful evangelical tool.

We have witnessed a significant creative period in contemporary Christian music over the past half century. In the wake of the Second Vatican Council and the adoption of the vernacular in the liturgy a flood of new music was created. Much of this music was written for congregational singing in the liturgy.

There has been another wave of new Christian music prompted particularly by the Charismatic Renewal in the Catholic Church and by contemporary expressions of evangelical faith and the rise of Pentecostalism. The focus of this music is not liturgical but rather it is music composed for communal worship. Such music gives expression to a desire to praise and glorify God. Its focus is on one's personal relationship with God. This new music appeals greatly to young people as its idiom is closely allied to modern musical genres. In one sense this music has "baptised" contemporary music styles. Such music has many close parallels with the psalms which expressed praise of God and captured poignant cries of the heart of the person of faith in the midst of the vicissitudes of life.

Worship music easily crosses denominational boundaries and songs can become universally popular. While songs that have come out of Pentecostal or evangelical churches can be quite appropriately used in non-liturgical settings for Catholics, there is a need for contemporary music written by Catholic composers who can evoke specific elements of Catholic spirituality, for example, devotion to the Blessed Sacrament.

There is now wide acceptance of the place of contemporary Christian music in the Church. It is useful to be able to identify various basic categories of contemporary compositions. Some have been composed for the liturgy and for use in Catholic devotional settings, like Adoration of the Blessed Sacrament. Other music has been composed for community singing at prayer meetings or rallies. Other music is appropriate more for a concert setting. It is important that contemporary music is used appropriately. It is also worth noting that some more traditional music can be very effective in more modern settings. It is interesting to note the recent interest among young people in Gregorian Chant.

Music now plays a vital role in many Catholic evangelical activities particularly for young people. Concerts, rallies, missions, prayer meetings all utilise contemporary Christian music as a means of giving expression to and stirring up the faith. Music can be used very effectively alongside kerygmatic preaching. It can help provide a prayerful setting for preaching and can be a vehicle to assist people in responding to the message.

Drama and the arts

Drama has also been proven to be a very successful tool for communicating with young people. Plays have been used since medieval times to convey spiritual messages. Drama has the ability to engage people. When the drama is a mime or a simple skit people are caught up not only in being entertained but by a curiosity as to the message.

Many mission teams which seek to reach out to youth use simple dramas to convey a religious message. The presentation of the drama can be followed by a testimony or discussion to bring out the meaning of the drama.

The Pontifical Council for Culture in a document entitled, "Towards a Pastoral Approach to Culture" commented that a world "increasingly obsessed with instant gratification, the lure of gain, the pursuit of profit and the overriding importance of possessions" is still attracted to beauty. It adds, "Intuitively, the Church was aware of this from its origins and centuries of Christian art magnificently illustrate this. Every true work of art is potentially a way into religious experience."[122]

Catholics are increasingly aware that art has a place in evangelisation and that it is beauty which speaks to the human spirit.

The Pontifical Council describes the power of art in these words:

> In showing how beautiful God is, the artist shows how much God is for man, as his own good and the ultimate truth of his existence. Christian beauty carries a truth bigger than the heart of man, truth that surpasses human language and indicates his good, the only essential.

Pope John Paul, in his *Letter to Artists*, spoke of a new *epiphany of beauty* and a new dialogue of faith and culture between Church and art.[123] On another occasion he spoke of the artistic patrimony inspired by the Christian faith as a "formidable instrument of catechesis", fundamental to "re-launch the universal message of beauty and good".[124]

---

122 Pontifical Council for Culture, *Towards a Pastoral Approach to Culture*, Art 17.
123 *Letter to Artists*, 4 April 1999.
124 Address to the Bishops of Tuscany, 11 March 1991.

Other associated arts all have a role to play in evangelisation. With the typical Hollywood film often conveying messages inimical to Christian faith and morality there is a need for Christian film-makers to produce commercially successful films which reflect a Christian view of life. Such films do not need to be overtly Christian but the messages they promote can accord with a Christian view of life.

There is a place, too, for popular writing which reflects Christian themes. Books by J.R.R. Tolkein and C.S. Lewis typify what can be achieved.

Catholic evangelisers have the opportunity to draw on the rich patrimony of Catholic art, architecture and music in presenting the beauty of the Christian Gospel to people of today.

Media

Media has a powerful influence in modern life. In all its forms – newspapers, magazines, radio, television, film and now the internet – its presence is pervasive and it therefore has enormous potential for evangelisation.

Media has been referred to as the "fourth estate". Journalists see their role as being independent investigators and commentators on social institutions. Thus the Catholic Church is often the object of investigative journalism and is often the object of criticism. The need for a stronger Catholic presence in the media is most needed. A Catholic well formed in faith can exercise significant influence by participating in the media.

The secular media is often hostile to the Church and it is able very often to influence public opinion. One very successful response to this situation has been Catholic Voices. It began with the aim to ensure that Catholics and the Church were well represented in the media when Pope Benedict came to the UK in September 2010. Catholic Voices trained 20 young professionals in media skills and organised intensive briefings on key issues which cause controversy in the media. It has gone on to be an effective Catholic presence in public debate in the UK.

New media

When America was discovered the Church was quick to send missionaries to bring the Gospel to peoples who had never heard of Christ. The result of their efforts is that the Americas are largely Christian today.

When we look at the spread of Christianity we can see how the Church was able to utilise the means of communication available at the time. What helped the initial spread of Christianity was the vast network of Roman roads. It meant that within the lifetime of the Apostles, the Gospel had been taken to the various parts of the Roman Empire, even to Gaul and Spain.

The Church has always made use of the media of the day to spread the Gospel. Monks devoted their lives to faithfully transcribing the sacred text and other great spiritual and theological works, enabling their dissemination. The Church became the great advocate of learning. Texts were translated into new languages as evangelists took the Gospel further and further afield. We honour Saints Cyril and Methodius for developing the Cyrillic alphabet in the ninth century, which enabled the Gospel to be taken to the Slavic peoples. The Church was able to embrace the new opportunities for mass production of written materials by utilising the printing press developed in the 15th century.

In more recent times radio offered a whole new possibility of universal communication. The popes were quick to begin to use it. Vatican Radio was established in 1931 and still continues today to communicate to a vast number of language groups. The advent of television saw great communicators like Archbishop Fulton Sheen reach out with Catholic teaching to people in their homes. Mother Angelica has been able to develop a worldwide television network – Eternal Word Television Network (EWTN) – beginning humbly in a garage.

In our times there are no new lands to be discovered, but there is a new virtual world being opened up through a range of extraordinary technological advances in communications. We are living through a communications revolution. It is an exciting time as advances are happening at increasing rates. It is also a time of great opportunity for the Church.

In recent years Pope Benedict in his World Communications Day Message emphasised the importance of engaging with the new media. In his 2009 Message he called young people who are most able to embrace and engage with the new media to use the opportunity to give witness to their faith and proclaim the Gospel within this new medium: "It falls, in particular, to young people, who have an almost spontaneous affinity for the new means of communication, to take on the responsibility for the evangelisation of this 'digital continent'."

In calling on young people to be involved in this new enterprise he commented on the fact that fruitful evangelisation required particular attention to the culture and customs of the people of the day. It is necessary not only to have the ability to use the new media, but also to know how to communicate through it to reach the people of today.

Such evangelisation of the digital continent needs digital evangelists. The Pope recognised this when he said to the young people he was inviting to become digital evangelists: "You know their fears and their hopes, their aspirations and their disappointments: the greatest gift you can give to them is to share with them the 'Good News' of a God who became man, who suffered, died and rose again to save all people." He knows that it will be young people themselves, filled with the faith and love of God, who will best evangelise the digital continent because they will best know and understand the needs of their peers.

Like missionaries who were often young themselves and set off to foreign lands to proclaim the Gospel, so in our day we need young missionaries who will devote themselves to using the new media to proclaim the Catholic faith.

The new media invites contemporary evangelisers to go to the virtual Areopagus. As described in Acts 17, St Paul went to the Areopagus as the place where ideas were shared and discussed. The Areopagus was the public square where people could come and listen. Now the public square is the World Wide Web which has two billion people participating. This is the new location for the Catholic faith to be proclaimed. This is the Areopagus of the third millennium.

One very good example of how new media for evangelisation is the work of Fr Robert Barron and his "Word on Fire" website. In an interview with *Our Sunday Visitor* he proposes seven tips for those who wish to evangelise in the new media.[125]

First, he says: "You must have a relationship with Jesus Christ. To evangelise is not just to share ideas — any theologian or historian could do that. It's to share a relationship, and you can't share what you don't have. Therefore, you've got to be in a personal relationship

---

[125] An interview with Brandon Vogt published in *Our Sunday Visitor* on 30 December 2012.

with the Lord Jesus Christ." Secondly: "You've got to be a person of ardour ... If you're not excited about your message, you won't communicate it effectively." The third point is that the evangelist must know Jesus within the context of salvation history.

As a fourth point he adds: "You've got to know the culture." He says: "When Pope John Paul called for 'new expressions', he was looking for new ways to express the faith to a secular society that has grown rather cold to the Gospel, and that has lost a sense of the transcendent. This requires you to look for 'seeds of the word'. Within the secular culture, there will always be signs, seeds and indications of the Gospel. So find these seeds, latch onto them, and engage the culture."

As his fifth point he says: "You've got to love the Great Tradition. We Catholics don't subscribe to sola Scriptura. We don't operate by Scripture alone. Scripture is the heart of theology, yes indeed, but as Blessed John Henry Newman said, it 'unfolds across space and time'. It's like a great river that continually broadens and deepens. We know Christ better because we know him through Augustine, Aquinas, Newman, Chesterton, and through Michelangelo and Dante. To know the great Catholic theological and artistic tradition is key to being a new evangelist."

Sixth, he says: "You've got to have a missionary heart." And finally his seventh point is: "You've got to know and use the new media. This explosion in technology is really unprecedented ... so use them and don't be afraid of technology."

Good advice from one who has become a leader in using the new media to promote the Gospel message.

It is worth offering a cautionary note into this new and fascinating field of new media. The technological advances in communications are fast and dramatic and we must not allow them to become ends in themselves. They are tools which can help us evangelise. We must not let our fascination with what is now technologically possible to get in the road of actually proclaiming the message. The most technically advanced production of something can be smart and innovative but not convey what we want to communicate. The medium must not overwhelm the message.

The other danger connected with the new media is that the virtual world cannot be allowed to replace the real world. In the end it will be interpersonal interaction that ensures evangelisation. Technology cannot of itself enable a person to come to faith. They need to come into a personal encounter with God.

All the Church's energies

In his encyclical on the mission of the Church, *Redemptoris Missio*, Pope John Paul made this striking statement: "I sense that the moment has come to commit all the Church's energies to a new evangelisation."[126] Evangelisation is not one among many priorities in the Church; it is not the domain of some interested in this field; it is not an optional extra. Evangelisation, as we have seen, is the very reason for the Church; it is its raison d'être; it is deepest identity. Thus, such a comment is not out of place or in any way extreme.

Evangelisation must be the centerpiece to all the Church's life and mission. Thus every work of the Church needs to be assessed in terms of its orientation towards evangelisation. Every person engaged with the life of the Church needs to ask how their participation in the Church is aiding its task of evangelisation.

It is thus appropriate that each and every organisation operating

---

126 *Redemptoris Missio*, n. 3.

in the name of the Church be able to identify its contribution to evangelisation. A Catholic hospital can ask how it is witnessing to the love of Christ and not just being a highly efficient medical facility. Every social agency needs to ask how people to whom it ministers know that it is the Christian faith that inspires its work. Every charitable work needs to be able to show how it presents the face of Christ in its activities. These works of the Church have come into being because of an encounter with Jesus Christ and "the love of Christ urges us on", as St Paul says.[127]

The Church is not a philanthropic institution. It is not a humanitarian organisation. It is not a social service agency. It is not focused on professional excellence as an end in itself. The Church does what it does because knowing Jesus Christ has so altered its approach to human life that it is inspired to self-sacrificing love and to an orientation towards the poor and needy. It is the example of Christ who came not to be served, but to serve that inspires the generous dedication and service to the suffering, the sick and the impoverished.

It is love that makes the difference to what the Church does. The Church has discovered love in and through Jesus Christ. The Church ministers the love of God for the world in its works. What is most important is that love not only inspires the Church's ministry but that this ministry brings others to know this love and understand its source. All the works of the Church need to be instruments by which

---

127 Pope Benedict released a *Motu Proprio* entitled "The Service of Charity" on 11 November 2012. In this document the Pope said that that "practical activity will always be insufficient, unless it visibly expresses a love for man, a love nourished by an encounter with Christ". In the light of this the document stated, "To ensure an evangelical witness in the service of charity, the diocesan Bishop is to take care that those who work in the Church's charitable apostolate, along with due professional competence, give an example of Christian life and witness to a formation of heart which testifies to a faith working through charity" (Art 7.2).

those it serves come to know God who is love, and they come to know Jesus Christ who is the incarnation of that love.

Fr Jules Chevalier, founder of the Daughters of our Lady of the Sacred Heart had a key catchphrase that inspired his life's work: "May the Sacred Heart of Jesus be everywhere loved." The Sisters ministered as missionaries and understood that their work was to enable people to discover the love within the Sacred Heart of Jesus.

Each Catholic institution and agency is being called upon to examine its works asking whether it has been effective in assisting people to know God in Jesus Christ. Thus, every agency of the Church is to be oriented around the fundamental mission of the Church – to proclaim Jesus Christ to the world.

12

Transforming the Culture

Christianity and culture

Human beings live within the context of a society which has elements that shape patterns of thought and action. Human beings live within and are influenced by the culture of their social setting. The surrounding culture can reflect a Christian vision of life, or be inimical to it. Today much of the Western world has inherited a culture shaped by Christianity which is now being changed by secular influences.

Evangelisation cannot only focus on the individual but must also consider how it is able influence the culture.

When Christianity came to the Roman Empire it performed perhaps one of the most significant cultural revolutions in Western civilisation. The Christian view of life stood directly opposed to the values promoted by classical thought expressed in the Greco-Roman tradition. In the centuries that followed the acceptance of Christianity within the Roman Empire the culture of Europe was changed. A Christian view of life influenced all dimensions of life. Indeed it is true that wherever Christian missionaries have penetrated they have had an impact on the cultures of the peoples among whom they have sought to evangelise.

The Catholic historian Christopher Dawson (1889-1970) argued that because the Christian faith embodies eternal values and the revelation of God, it is able to transform the cultures it comes into contact with. When the Christian faith enters into a culture, as it did with Rome, it begins a spiritual regeneration of that culture. In an essay entitled "The Christian View of History", Dawson wrote:

> For the Christian doctrine of the Incarnation is not simply a theophany — a revelation of God to Man; it is a new creation – the introduction of a new spiritual principle which gradually leavens and transforms human nature into something new. The history of the human race hinges on this unique divine event which gives meaning to the whole historical process.

Dawson wrote on the subject of culture because he understood that European culture, grounded as it was in Christianity, was beginning to undergo what he called a "cultural discontinuity". He spoke of modern positivism sapping the culture its moral underpinnings. He saw the threat of a new emerging culture that lacked a basic narrative.

Dawson saw that there was a moral basis to Christian society. In his book, *Understanding Europe*, Dawson observed:

> If we are to make the ordinary man aware of the spiritual unity out of which all the separate activities of our civilization have arisen, it is necessary in the first place to look at Western civilization as a whole and to treat it with the same objective appreciation and respect which the humanists of the past devoted to the civilisation of antiquity.

He understood that European society, which has influenced many other nations, emerged because of a common faith which had fostered a moral vision for human life.

Dawson saw, as St Augustine expressed it, that there was a conflict between the City of God and the City of Man in every age. He was aware that the respect for human dignity and individual freedom was threatened by various expressions of godless society. For Dawson this was evident in Nazism and Communism. Under such collectivist societies personal moral effort and the assumption of responsibility for one's actions can be overwhelmed. The person becomes a mere cog in the machine of the state. At the present time we could view this threat to culture in the rise of secularism. Secularism is capable of effecting what Pope Benedict has described as a "dictatorship of relativism"[128] which robs the human person of the dignity of moral responsibility.

Christianity enabled the formation of a civilisation which provided a stable social structure underpinned by supernatural reality. Societies molded by Christianity have much to offer the contemporary world. Bringing the Gospel to all nations provides the opportunity for cultures to be enriched as they discover the essential dignity of each human being. It is this understanding of the nature of the human person that promotes personal freedom, protection of the sacredness of human life and secures a true recognition of the nature of marriage and family.

It is in this light that we can understand the insistence of Pope John Paul that the Church propose a "culture of life"[129] in the face of a growing "culture of death", and his vision of a "Civilisation of Love".[130]

Christopher Dawson commented in an unpublished manuscript

---

128 See homily of Joseph Cardinal Ratzinger, Dean of the College of Cardinals, in the Mass for the Election of the Supreme Pontiff, St Peter's Basilica, 18 April 2005. Pope Francis affirmed this phrase in his address to the Diplomatic Corps accredited to the Holy See, 22 March 2013.
129 Pope John Paul II first used the phrase "culture of life" in a World Youth Day tour of the United States in 1993. Speaking to journalists at Stapleton International Airport near Denver, Colorado, the Pope denounced abortion and euthanasia, stating that: "The culture of life means respect for nature and protection of God's work of creation." He used this theme in his encyclical, *Evangelium Vitae*, 25 March 1995.
130 Following Pope Paul VI's use of the phrase "Civilisation of Love" – firstly on Pentecost Sunday, 1970 – Pope John Paul II's first public address as pope mentioned the phrase. By the end of 2003 the phrase has been used in some 208 papal documents.

(1928): "Every culture is like a plant. It must have its roots in the earth, and for sunlight it needs to be open to the spiritual. At the present moment we are busy cutting its roots and shutting out all light from above." [131] His conviction was that culture needed two elements: the human and the transcendent. Culture that would promote human flourishing needs to be inspired by faith.

Every person exists within a culture and that culture has a significant influence on the person's view of life. In a work which explored the nature of culture, the Pontifical Council for Culture stated that culture includes "the whole of human activity, human intelligence and emotions, the human quest for meaning, human customs and ethics". It adds, "Culture is so natural to man that human nature can only be revealed through culture."[132] Thus evangelisation cannot ignore the influence of culture and seek to effect the transformation of culture by the Christian Gospel.

In this present age, culture inspired by a transcendental vision is seriously at risk. Pope Paul commented that "the split between the Gospel and culture is without a doubt the drama of our time, just as it was of other times".[133] The Pope spoke of the need to bring the Gospel to influence "all the strata of society" and thus "transforming humanity from within and making it new". The Church sees its role as not only leading individuals to Christ, but to bring about the evangelisation of culture.

Pope Benedict explained that the evangelisation of culture is in the long run at the service of the culture:

---

131 Quoted in a forward by Christina Scott to *Progress and Religion: an Historical Inquiry* (the collected works of Christopher Dawson). 1929.
132 *Towards a Pastoral Approach to Culture*, Pontifical Council for Culture 1999 n. 2.
133 Pope Paul VI, *Evangelii Nuntiandi*, 8 December 1975, n. 20.

The evangelisation of culture is all the more important in our times, when a "dictatorship of relativism" threatens to obscure the unchanging truth about man's nature, his destiny and his ultimate good. There are some who now seek to exclude religious belief from public discourse, to privatise it or even to paint it as a threat to equality and liberty. Yet religion is in fact a guarantee of authentic liberty and respect, leading us to look upon every person as a brother or sister.[134]

Shaping the culture

The Church must be present not only to individuals but to the culture. Catholic evangelisation must include initiatives to influence the culture. The first step in influencing the culture is to have a presence in society. There is pressure for the Church to keep its views to itself among its own people. Pope Benedict focused on this explicitly in his address at Westminster Hall responding to this issue in the United Kingdom. He said that religion is a "vital contributor to the national conversation". He made specific reference to the fact that even in countries which have a tradition of tolerance there are those who advocate that the voice of religion should be silenced.[135]

As a contributor to the national conversation Christians are advocates for life, for family, for the dignity and rights of the individual. It is the role of Christians to seek to evangelise the culture by being advocates of truth and to promote the pursuit of truth as offering the right foundation for social cohesion and human flourishing.

We have already spoken of some areas in which the Church

---

134 Pope Benedict XVI Homily at Mass in Scotland, 16 September 2010.
135 Address to Politicians, Diplomats, Academics and Business Leaders, Westminster Hall, 17 September 2010.

needs to be present and active. To begin to reclaim the culture for Christianity some particular areas of activity are important:

- The media.
- The arts.
- Dialogue between faith and reason.
- Witness to sacredness of human life.
- Promotion of the Christian view of marriage and family.
- Engagement in the public square.

The evangelisation of culture falls in a particular way to lay people who operate within the professional, social and political life of the society. They have a mission to contribute to society through the inspiration of their Catholic faith.

Changes in the urban environment

Culture takes a concrete expression in the physical environment in which we live. We will now examine the changes that have occurred in the concrete shape of our urban and suburban life and how these changes have impacted on Christian life.

The presence of the Church in the urban setting has significantly changed with the rapid urbanisation of modern life. In the great cities of Europe the cathedral has a commanding presence. They are often at the very heart of the city. In medieval times they were structures that dominated the cityscape. Their spires would reach well above any other building pointing to the heavens. They were works not only of massive size but also of great natural beauty. Both from without and within they were striking testimony to the citizenry of transcendental realities. The era of the great cathedrals bore eloquent testimony of the centrality of faith not only to personal life, but to the life of the city. Cathedrals were centres of culture and locations of key civic events.

This has now significantly changed. Where cathedrals and major churches still exist within the heart of the city, they are often now dwarfed by commercial buildings. Huge office towers testify to the achievement of man. They are symbols of financial and commercial success. The cityscape now gives glory to the achievements of man.

These evident changes in the architecture of our major cities also reflect what has in fact happened to the place of the Church in daily life of citizens in the great metropolis. Evidence of faith has been pushed to the margins of life. The buzz and vitality of city life now catches people's attention. Cities are places not only of business but also of entertainment. Cities now construct entertainment precincts. City life – particularly its night life – is now dominated by the activities of man. Living in modern urban environments all the signs around promote the values of a life without God.

Living and working in urban environments it is hard to find any witness to the presence of Christianity. All the signs, the advertising, the lights, promote the life of man. There is little or nothing to witness to spiritual things. In the cities it seems as though God is absent.

Penetrating the urban environment

How can we address the challenge that religion has been pushed to the sidelines in modern urban life? Often in the CBD there are a number of churches, dwarfed by the office towers. They are refuges for the faithful. City churches offer Masses and Confessions serving city workers. This is an important service. However they are ignored by the throngs of people passing their doors.

City churches do attract the searching and the desperate. They often provide charitable services for the needy who congregate in the urban centres. They can provide a tangible witness to Christian charity.

However, it is not enough that they provide some services for those who seek them.

City churches can become centres for evangelisation. Their presence in places where multitudes of people come for work or entertainment offer the possibility of evangelical outreach. A city parish has the capacity to be an effective missionary presence in the city. City churches can orient their ministry to reach out to the crowds who throng the streets.

City churches can firstly give clear sign that they are open for people to visit. As well as offering sacramental services a city church can provide various opportunities for prayer and spiritual nourishment. Imaginative ways can attract people off the streets. The visible presence of a priest can offer people an opportunity for spiritual counsel.

City churches can offer a variety of means for people to seek God.

Evangelisers associated with city church can become an active presence among the people. The Church needs to go out onto the streets. Evangelisers can stand outside the church and hand out Christian literature. A city parish could organise religious processions which give public witness to faith.

Modern urban centres are locations for many festivals and celebrations. City leaders are often supportive of community events as they attract people to the city and build the reputation of the city as an attractive location. This can be an area where the Church can become active. Our celebrations can be taken into the marketplace. Christmas and Easter are important opportunities to be publicly active. Catholic festivals can be held in the cathedral precincts and promoted in such a way as to attract people to attend. Concerts, expos and cultural events can give witness to the vitality of the Catholic faith.

The ringing of church bells on Sunday can be a reminder to the citizens that Sunday is the Lord's Day and people are attending the Church.

It is possible for a diocese to conduct a "City Mission" which reaches out into the CBD. Events of the mission can be conducted in venues around the city and not only within the cathedral or city churches. It is important that the Church has a clear visibility in large urban centres.

Such activities give testimony to the city that the Church is alive and active. In its evangelising work Catholics do not seek to be aggressive or confrontational. We seek to attract and inspire rather than demand and argue.

Such activities often bring great heart to ordinary Catholics. They are proud of seeing their Church presenting itself unashamedly to the society. For those who become involved it is a source of the strengthening of their faith.

Suburban life

What has occurred in the urban centres has been matched by significant changes in suburban life. In times past the churches were built close to the heart of a suburban village. We often see streets named "Church Street" because this was the street in which there were a number of churches.

The parish church was readily accessible to people. They would pass it going to the shops. They could wander down for a parish event. In European culture there was often a piazza in front of the church and the church offered a backdrop to weekly markets, cultural events and simply standing around talking, or sipping coffee alfresco.

In earlier times in Australian society where Catholics were a minority and life was slower and simpler, the parish provided a natural centre for community life. As well as providing Mass and Sacraments and various spiritual activities the parish organised regular social events. Life for many Catholics naturally revolved around the local parish.

Cities like Sydney went through a significant change in character in the post-WWII period. It was a time of rapid growth. This new growth was coupled with the ability of the average family to own a car. New possibilities for mobility introduced the possibility of what has come to known as the urban sprawl with its dormitory suburbs and quarter acre block. Large areas of land were opened up for development. Sydney spread right across the basin determined by the Blue Mountains, the Hawkesbury River and Port Hacking.

The Church struggled to keep up as it built new parish complexes of church, presbytery and school. It became more and more necessary to build away from the suburban centre of the shops and railway station. The link between the parish and the local community changed.

The parish was still an important centre especially with the parish primary school linking families to the parish site. However, people's lives were changing. People were more mobile. Life was busier. The parish ceased to be a community centre and became more a service centre – a place that provided Mass, the Sacraments, and education.

It has become harder for parishes to preserve the spirit of being a close knit community. Many comment now that they feel anonymous at Mass. People today come to the parish for the fulfilment of personal spiritual needs. They come to Mass and go home. People will shop around for a parish that suits them rather than the parish where they live. It might be the liturgy, or the priest or the parking that attracts them to participate in another parish. Loyalty to one's parish is far more tenuous today.

Priests find it harder and harder to engage people in the life of a parish apart from coming to the parish to get what they need. The consumer mentality is strong in the life of many Catholics. This simply is a reflection of the changes in culture. With busy and demanding lives people look to parishes more as agencies that provide certain services that they need. They go to the supermarket to shop, to the petrol station for fuel, to the parish for their spiritual needs.

While we may have an ideal for what a parish is meant to be, the reality of the parish today is due to many factors beyond the control of the Church. This is not helped by the growing secularisation of our society.

The parish in Catholic life

The parish is and will remain a vital aspect of the life of the Church and will continue to be the locus for Catholic life. As such it needs special consideration in relation to evangelisation.

The parish is the concrete expression of the Church for the Catholic and is the location of the celebration of key sacramental moments in the pilgrimage of faith. Catholics naturally relate their life of faith to the parish. It is the place of baptism and confirmation, of the receiving of First Holy Communion (and First Reconciliation). It is the place for the celebration of the Sacrament of Marriage, and the place from which a Catholic is taken for Christian burial. Thus, the parish plays a vital role for the Catholic.

In his encyclical addressed to lay people, *Christifideles Laici,* Pope John Paul acknowledged that while the Church always has a universal dimension, it "finds its most immediate and visible expression in the parish". People experience what it means to belong to the Church, above all, in terms of their relationship with the parish community in which they live.

It is also a key location for formation in our faith. In Australia parishes have supported and developed a very impressive system of primary and secondary schools. Primary schools in particular are integral to the life of the parish and usually occupy the same piece of land where the church is built. Primary school children are naturally oriented around the parish church and the parish priest. This helps them build their Catholic identity.

Formation in faith is also provided for adults in a wide variety of ways in and through the parish. The Sunday homily is an immediate source not only of spiritual nourishment, but also of the ongoing formation of understanding of the faith. Various groups meet in the parish and offer formation in Catholic faith, such as Lenten groups, prayer groups and bible study groups.

The parish is a community of believers. Thus Catholics living in the secular and at times unfriendly environment of contemporary society find support and encouragement from fellow parishioners. In this regard the witness of the faith and Christian life of fellow parishioners can be of great importance. Life in contemporary society offers so few inspirations to Christian ideals. Catholics today can feel isolated and alone in what they believe and how they want to live. The parish community is a welcome refuge and a source of encouragement.

The strength of a parish is to be found in the quality of the life of the members of the parish living and co-operating together. Parishioners can discover a basic biblical truth: we are brothers and sisters to each other in Christ. Because of the common baptism and the life of the Spirit that Catholics share, "we belong to one another", as St Paul says (Romans 12:5). Today, more than ever, the Catholic faithful need each other.

Pope John Paul in *Christifideles Laici* expressed the hope that "in the light of faith all rediscover the true meaning of the parish, that is, the place where the very mystery of the Church is present and at work". He stresses that "the parish is not principally a structure, a territory, or a building, but rather "the family of God, a fellowship afire with a unifying spirit, a familiar and welcoming home, the community of the faithful. Plainly and simply the parish is founded on a theological reality, because it is a Eucharistic community". The Pope added:

> This means that the parish is a community properly suited for celebrating the Eucharist, the living source for its upbuilding and the sacramental bond of its being in full communion with the whole Church. Such suitableness is rooted in the fact that the parish is a *community of faith* and an *organic community*, that is, constituted by the ordained ministers and other Christians, in which the pastor – who represents the diocesan bishop – is the hierarchical bond with the entire particular Church.[136]

Thus, when we come to consider the task of evangelisation, the parish is to play a vital role. However, we must understand the current reality of parishes as has been described above. Older approaches no longer work. The changes in the circumstances of parishes offer particular challenge when it comes to evangelisation. In times past

---

136 *Christifideles Laici*, n. 26.

parish missions, for instance, would be conducted within the Catholic community. Effort would be made to visit those Catholics who were not regular attendees at the parish. Parish missions would be well attended. They were occasions for the spiritual renewal of the parish. They worked well.

Now parish missions are much more difficult to conduct. Attendances are low. It is not just disinterest in religion. The sheer pace of life discourages many from fully participating. We need to look at new ways to evangelise both within the parish community and then beyond it to the local geographical area.

Parish Missions

We have spoken previously about parish missions as one of the important instruments for the new evangelisation. As we are speaking about renewing parishes it is worth returning to the issue. As we have noted, parish missions in the past reached out to Catholics both practicing and non-practicing. In their day they were very successful. Now with changed times we need to find new ways of doing things.

Parish mission now have to take direction from the call to the new evangelisation. Such missions will be different in style as they seek to be as much conducted "in the marketplace" as in the church building. The use of pubs or clubs are means of bringing the mission to the people.

There are, of course, activities that take place in the church, particularly the key spiritual activities but these missions need to reach out to people where they are. So those conducting the mission need to go into the shopping centres, to be on the streets, visiting homes and schools.

Such missions are best conducted by a team which should include a priest, but may include a number of lay people. The mission team needs to be clearly identifiable. These days the coloured tee shirt with suitable "branding" is often used, particularly by younger missionaries. Such missions hold a wide range of events which often a good number of people to help organise and present. A team presence with the mission is often very helpful as individual members are able to engage with different people in the course of the mission.

A mission in the new evangelisation has a very distinctive character. Music, drama, the arts and well as innovative ways of gaining people's attention are important means to reach out to people who may have little association with things spiritual.

It is recommended that parishes conduct a mission once every three years. Parish missions in the new evangelisation should become a regular feature of the parish's effort to evangelise the local community. Having regular missions enables the parish community to continue to focus on its own spiritual renewal and also to have an orientation towards the wider community.

Parishes on an evangelisation footing

If, as I am proposing, the new evangelisation is to become the pastoral focus for the Church at this time, the beginning of the third millennium, then parishes need to orient themselves towards this goal. Parishes need to become evangelising centres in their own right.

Such a focus means that the parish community develops an evangelising vision. Priest and people would begin to work together in developing plans to evangelise the community in which they are embedded.

There are a number of works of the parish which readily lend themselves to this task.

The RCIA is an obvious tool. Those involved in the RCIA team need to be promoters of evangelisation and set up pathways for people who show interest in the faith.

The local Catholic school offers potential. There are many parents who are not practicing the faith or are not Catholic themselves but are well disposed to the Church through their involvement in the local Catholic school. Imaginative ways to reach out to them and offer ways to connect with the life of the parish can be explored. Having a person appointed to be a link between parish and school can assist in facilitating this.

Various spiritual groups should be encouraged to have an outward looking orientation. Prayer groups, bible study groups, Legion of Mary and many other organisations which are often part of parish life can be imbued with an evangelical spirit.

It is possible to establish small groups who meet to pray and be formed in Christian living. These groups can be based on a cell model whereby they seek to grow with new members and at a certain size break into two groups.

Parishes can conduct regular functions focused on evangelisation. Parishes can invite evangelistic speakers, hold special prayer events, and have evangelistic music concerts, all of which are aimed at reaching out to those away from the faith and the Church.

Each parish council should appoint a small committee to drive its evangelising activity.

In their document promoting evangelisation, *Go and Make Disciples*, the American bishops emphasised:

> Every element of the parish must respond to the evangelical imperative – priests, religious, lay persons, parish staff, ministers, organisations, social clubs, local schools and parish

religious education programmes. Otherwise evangelisation will be something a few people in the parish see as their ministry – rather than the reason for the parish's existence *and the objective of every ministry in the parish.*[137]

Schools as centres for evangelisation

Catholic schools are very important elements in the evangelising mission of the Church. The cultural milieu in which Catholic schools operate has changed significantly in recent decades and Catholic schools need to reconfigure themselves to meet new challenges.

The Catholic Church has always understood that the primary responsibility for education rests with parents. Parents choose to send their children to Catholic schools because they support the nature of the education offered by the schools. While many may not place religious formation as the highest of their desires, still many believe that the Catholic character of the school is a positive quality in their child's education.

Catholic schools in many parts of the Western world are coming under various pressures from governments particularly as government funding has become vital for the sustainability of Catholic schools. Governments seek to have more direct influence on the education offered at the schools by exercising greater influence over curriculum. This has been evidenced in Australia by the development of a National Curriculum. This intervention in the actual content of education, while understandable from the point of view of ensuring consistent content in education in Australian society, can inhibit the freedom of Catholic schools to present a Catholic perspective and reflect the Catholic intellectual tradition.

---

137 *Go and Make Disciples*, n. 85.

The 1998 Vatican document, *The Catholic School on the Threshold of the Third Millennium*, addressed the issue of the pressure on Catholic schools to embrace a certain neutrality, denying the freedom of Catholic schools to reflect their distinctive character. It stated:

> The fragmentation of education, the generic character of the values frequently invoked and which obtain ample and easy consensus at the price of a dangerous obscuring of their content, tend to make the school step back into a supposed neutrality, which enervates its educating potential and reflects negatively on the formation of the pupils. There is a tendency to forget that education always presupposes and involves a definite concept of man and life. To claim neutrality for schools signifies in practice, more times than not, banning all reference to religion from the cultural and educational field, whereas a correct pedagogical approach ought to be open to the more decisive sphere of ultimate objectives, attending not only to "how", but also to "why", overcoming any misunderstanding as regards the claim to neutrality in education, restoring to the educational process the unity which saves it from dispersion amid the meandering of knowledge and acquired facts, and focuses on the human person in his or her integral, transcendent, historical identity. With its educational project inspired by the Gospel, the Catholic school is called to take up this challenge and respond to it in the conviction that "it is only in the mystery of the Word made flesh that the mystery of man truly becomes clear".[138]

Catholic schools experience other challenges. The most recognised issue at present is the lack of adequate formation in faith of many

---

[138] *The Catholic School on the Threshold of the Third Millennium*, 10 (the final quote is from *Gaudium et Spes*, 22).

teachers. In the religious formation programmes, teachers who are not committed to the Catholic faith are required by circumstances to teach the religious education curriculum. They do this while lacking the personal conviction about the content. Students are able to see that their teachers do not really believe what they are teaching.

The effective formation of teachers who will teach the Catholic faith is a critical priority for Catholic schools.

It is also true that many Catholic schools can no longer rely on the religious socialisation as a means of nourishing the faith of students. In times past Catholic schools provided a rich environment of faith which fostered a sense of faith among the students. Indeed it is true today that peer pressure at school can actively work against the transmission of faith.

The creation of a positive atmosphere of Catholic faith is a real challenge facing Catholic education authorities.

Educational theory concerning handing on the faith has promoted the notion that the school has the role of providing religious education. It has been argued that it is not the role of the teacher to try to influence students, but merely provide the materials whereby students gain a degree of religious literacy. According to this theory it is the role of the parish to catechise young people when they seek to receive the various sacraments of initiation.

Catholic schools have traditionally seen their role as far more than this. Catholic schools have been key agents for the nourishment of personal faith. The religious who devoted their lives to Catholic education saw their role as one of directly nurturing the faith of their students. Religious education in our schools cannot just be the transmission of information about the faith, there is a need for a kerygmatic catechesis to call the students to faith. It is essential that all teachers who teach religion are themselves committed to the faith.

In an era when religious beliefs and practises are increasingly marginalised there is a need for a reappraisal of how the faith is articulated and nurtured in schools. A reconceptualisation of religious education is now needed.[139]

In 2010 the Catholic Bishops of NSW/ACT released a document entitled *Catholic Schools at a Crossroads*. This document addressed the question of making schools agents of the new evangelisation and proposed a set of criteria for this to occur.

It said that if Catholic schools are to be centres of the new evangelisation then the following is required:

- the life and activity in the school would be the context for a personal encounter with Christ and would promote, and never contradict, the teachings of the Church;
- all those involved in our schools would appreciate their roles in receiving and proclaiming the Good News by word and deed, and by the example of their lives;
- students would participate in RE classes, liturgies, retreats and prayers which are, as far as possible, tailored to their place in the journey of faith, addressing the core of our faith and inviting a response;
- special programmes would be developed for students who first enter a Catholic school later than Kindergarten (for instance in Year 7) and may not have received much prior religious education;
- schools would work with their local parish(es) to establish programmes for initiating children and young adults into the Church.

---

[139] See Richard Rymarz, *The New Evangelisation, Issues and Challenges for Catholic Schools*. Modotti Press, 2012.

- other efforts would be pursued to integrate the activity of our primary and secondary schools with the life of the surrounding parish(es) and diocese, so that our young people are given a sense of belonging to a wider Church beyond their family and school;
- every effort would be made to engage our students and young teachers in preparations for, participation in and enrichment after major religious events such as World Youth Day; and
- families and parishes would support their schools in all these activities.

The bishops called on all Catholic educational leaders, staff and parents, as well as the broader Catholic community, to join them in recommitting to Catholic schooling in the new situation of the 21st century. They challenged all those involved to dedicate themselves to ensuring that our schools are truly Catholic in their identity and life and become centres of the new evangelisation.

At the Synod of Bishops on the New Evangelisation, held in 2012, the topic of Catholic schools arose, noting that they are well-positioned instruments for the new evangelisation. In the document publishing the "Final List of Propositions" from the Synod, one of the propositions said that "education is a constitutive dimension of evangelisation". It added, "To proclaim the risen Jesus Christ is to accompany all human beings in their personal story, in their development and in their spiritual vocation." The bishops said that education needs "to promote everything that is true, good and beautiful that is part of the human person, that is to say, to educate the mind and the emotions to appreciate reality". The Synod Fathers said that it is important that our educational institutions not just be "products of evangelisation", but "agents of evangelisation".

Catholic identity of schools

As Pope Benedict pointed out, "Education is integral to the mission of the Church to proclaim the good news. First and foremost, every Catholic institution is a place to encounter the Living God who in Jesus Christ reveals His transforming love and truth." Catholic education is one of the great works of the Church. In Australia we have a proud history of achievement in offering Catholic education to the young. Our first canonised saint, St Mary of the Cross MacKillop, captures the spirit of dedication to Catholic education.

The Pope's words quoted above very usefully summarise the goal of Catholic education. The schools should facilitate an encounter with Jesus Christ. This implies that the schools not only teach about Christ but offer an opportunity to actually encounter Him. The Pope is proposing that students have a profound faith experience whereby they come to know Christ in an intimate way.

This goal has much relevance at this moment in history. We know that many young people do not have a living faith. They may have some vague sense of the spiritual – the cry today is "I am spiritual but not religious". This view, though, reduces faith to a matter of personal preference. To be content to have some vague spiritual sense of things does not do justice to what the Catholic faith is and the way it is meant to shape our lives. The Catholic faith is far more profound than that.

This is the great challenge before all those involved in Catholic education. Catholic schools exist to form young people in the faith and to provide a faith-based environment for their education. In cooperation and partnership with parents, the first educators of their children, these schools seek to educate the whole child by providing an excellent education. The distinguishing feature of this education is its underpinning in Catholic doctrine and life.

We can recognise some key indicators which would guide educators as to whether their school was on track. These indicators include:

Catholic Identity: Catholic primary and secondary schools should unashamedly profess their Catholic identity and this identity should find expression in the daily life of the school. Catholic schools are evidently Catholic in their "look and feel". The presence of Catholic symbols is important: crucifixes, statues, holy pictures should all be in evidence. Sacred Scripture should be frequently quoted in school publications. The school motto should be identifiably Catholic. The celebration of the Church's liturgical year should be integrated into the rhythm of school life.

Evangelising Mission: A Catholic school would embrace the evangelising mission of the Church. It has as its goal assisting every student to come to know Christ in a personal way. It faithfully transmits Catholic teaching in its integrity. The school would also be aware of its role in assisting families to live the faith in the home. The school, in fact, can be an instrument in fostering a deeper faith in the lives of the parents.

Spiritual Formation: Catholic schools shall provide appropriate occasions for prayer, liturgical worship, and the celebration of the Sacraments of Reconciliation and the Eucharist to foster the spiritual formation of students. It is important that the students (and also parents) have regular exposure to moments of prayer. Prayer fosters an awareness of the divine and helps people enter the realm of the Spirit.

Religious Instruction: Priority is given to ensure that students receive a systematic instruction in the Catholic faith. This instruction does not avoid the harder issues but presents the Catholic tradition in such a way that students are attracted to its essential truth and beauty. Catholic schools need to ensure that not only is there provision for a sound and thorough presentation of the Catholic faith in the times designated for religious instruction, but that other subjects include reference to the Catholic faith.

Religion Teachers: Religion teachers should be practicing Catholics, qualified to teach religion. They shall have a deep knowledge of and a desire to hand on the authentic Catholic faith. They should live as authentic witnesses to the faith. The adage is true: you cannot give what you have not got. To this end, the ongoing formation of teachers and opportunities for them to deepen their faith should be seen as a priority.

Relationship with Priests and Parishes: Catholic schools need to maintain a close relationship with local priests and parishes. Students should be encouraged to participate in the life of their parish. Efforts are made to liaise with parishes and find creative ways of engaging students and their families in parish life.

Communion and Cooperation with the Bishop: Catholic schools have a formal and defined relationship with the bishop of the diocese who has oversight of the teaching of the faith in all Catholic schools. This relationship is vital to maintain communion within the Church. It is important that teachers understand that in the end they are to be in real communion with the bishop in all that they do in their schools.

These key indicators are a way in which a Catholic school can assess its engagement with the mission of the Church. These indicators provide a basis whereby a Catholic school is part of the new evangelisation.

13

New Springtime

Evangelisation is the pastoral priority for the Church for the beginning of the third millennium. The task before the Church is to lead people to come to know Jesus Christ in a personal way. This is the unchanging mission of the Church. In our time this vision of the Christian life is being renewed led by the teaching of the Popes. They have understood that this must be the priority for all aspects of the life and mission of the Church. It is also evident in the Church that there is a movement towards this goal. It is being stimulated particularly by the emergence of many new communities and movements. They have been responsible for the revitalisation of the faith of many millions of Catholics and they have implanted in the mission of the Church new and effective ways in which the evangelising mission can be carried out.

The Synod of Bishops in 2012 said in one of its propositions: "At its heart the New Evangelisation is the re-proposing of the encounter with the risen Lord, his Gospel and his Church to those who no longer find the Church's message engaging." To achieve this all members of the Church need to have a personal experience of the living Christ and then, renewed and reinvigorated in their personal faith, have a burning desire – "ardour" is the word used by Pope John Paul – to share that experience with others.

The new ardour that is needed requires this personal spiritual renewal. A new focus on evangelisation cannot not be achieved by the implementation of various programmes or methods without the inner spiritual vigour which can only come from a heart touched by the love and power of God. As Pope John Paul urged, "We must rekindle in ourselves the impetus of the beginnings and allow ourselves to be filled with the ardour of the apostolic preaching which followed Pentecost. We must revive in ourselves the burning conviction of Paul, who cried out: 'Woe to me if I do not preach the Gospel'."[140]

The Church is discovering that there are many new methods that can be used to evangelise. We are experiencing an exciting period of fresh imagination and innovation as those with a passion to proclaim their faith are doing so in surprising and effective ways.

Catholics are exploring all sorts of new means of expressing the Christian message. The new technologies are being ulitised such as the internet, video, social media and radio. The more traditional forms of communication like mime, drama, music and the arts are all being explored and used to good effect.

We can see signs of a new springtime, even if the buds are still small and the full flowering is still some way off. However, the winter is over and the spring is upon us.

We have been urged on in this by our recent popes. We have seen ample evidence of their understanding of the importance of the new evangelisation for the future of the Church. Pope John Paul has on many occasions been quite bold in his statements. His words in *Redemptoris Missio* stand out: "I sense that the moment has come to commit *all* of the Church's energies to the new evangelisation ... No believer in Christ, no institution of the Church can avoid this supreme duty: to proclaim Christ to all peoples."[141]

---

140 *Novo Millennio Ineunte*, n. 40.
141 *Redemptoris Missio*, n. 3.

The role of the Holy Spirit

However, the principal agent of evangelisation is the Holy Spirit, as Pope Paul so eloquently noted in *Evangelii Nuntiandi*: "Evangelisation will never be possible without the action of the Holy Spirit." He continued:

> Techniques of evangelisation are good, but even the most advanced ones could not replace the gentle action of the Spirit. The most perfect preparation of the evangeliser has no effect without the Holy Spirit. Without the Holy Spirit, the most convincing dialectic has no power over the heart of man. Without Him the most highly developed schemas resting on a sociological or psychological basis are quickly seen to be quite valueless.[142]

Like his predecessor, Pope John Paul had confidence that it will be the Holy Spirit at work in the Church who will ultimately inspire and make fruitful its evangelising mission:

> The horizons and possibilities for mission are growing ever wider, and we Christians are called to an apostolic courage based upon trust in the Spirit. *He is the principal agent of mission*!
>
> The history of humanity has known many major turning points which have encouraged missionary outreach, and the Church, guided by the Spirit, has always responded to them with generosity and farsightedness. Results have not been lacking.[143]

---

142 *Evangelii Nuntiandi*, n. 75.
143 *Redemptoris Missio*, n. 30.

The joy of evangelising

Evangelisation is the call, the task, the duty of all Catholics, but it is also the joy of living the Christian life. The Christian knows that they have a treasure in their Christian faith. This faith has proven itself to be a constant source of encouragement, of hope and of joy. We can live our lives in the joy of the Lord.

What we offer to the world is the joy of knowing God and living under the hand of his love.

Pope Paul concluded his great document on evangelisation with these words: "Let us therefore preserve our fervour of spirit. Let us preserve the delightful and comforting joy of evangelising, even when it is in tears that we must sow".

He then adds:

> And may the world of our time, which is searching, sometimes with anguish, sometimes with hope, be enabled to receive the Good News not from evangelisers who are dejected, discouraged, impatient or anxious, but from ministers of the Gospel whose lives glow with fervour, who have first received the joy of Christ, and who are willing to risk their lives so that the kingdom may be proclaimed and the Church established in the midst of the world.[144]

---

144 *Evangelii Nuntiandi*, n. 80.

Afterword

During the course of my writing this book Pope Benedict XVI convoked a Synod on the subject of the *New Evangelisation for the Transmission of the Christian Faith*. It was held in Rome in October 2012. On the Feast of Christ the King in the year 2013, to conclude the Year of Faith, Pope Francis promulgated his Apostolic Exhortation based on the Synod under the title *Evangelii Gaudium*, the Joy of the Gospel.

This writing of Pope Francis captures many of the outcomes of the Synod which were put together in a list of fourteen propositions. The exhortation reflects the unique style of Pope Francis and contains many of his own insights into evangelisation. Pope Francis had given a good deal of attention to the subject. He was charged to draft a document on the mission of the Church in South America following the fifth general conference of the Bishops of South America. This document, often referred to as the *Aparecida Document* was promulgated in 2007. One sees echoes of the document in many sections of *Evangelii Gaudium*.

The very title of the exhortation reflects the spirit of Pope Francis, he speaks about the joy of that is discovered by knowing Jesus Christ. His opening sentences read: "The joy of the Gospel fills the hearts and lives of all who encounter Jesus. Those who accept his offer of salvation are set free from sin, sorrow, inner emptiness and loneliness. With Christ joy is constantly born anew."[145] He invites Christians "everywhere, at this very moment, to a renewed personal encounter with Jesus Christ, or at least an openness to letting him encounter

---
145 *Evangelii Gaudium*, n. 1.

them".[146] Clearly Pope Francis knows that evangelisation can only become a living reality in the Church when members of the Church open their lives to him in a way that enables a real encounter to occur.

The exhortation reflects much of the teaching of the previous popes. Pope Francis states: "We should realise that missionary outreach is paradigmatic for all the Church's activity."[147] On this basis he then quotes from the *Aparecida Document* in reminding us that the Church "cannot passively and calmly wait in our church buildings". He echoes the document in adding that the Church must move from pastoral ministry of mere conservation to a decidedly missionary pastoral ministry.[148] Pope Francis has used some bold statements to urge the Church to move beyond its own comfortable and safe confines and to reach out to people, particularly those on the margins. He encourages priests to move "out of the sacristy" and bishops not to spend too much time away from the diocese. He spoke to a group of newly appointed bishops and warned them to "avoid the scandal of being airport bishops". In all he calls on the clergy to move out among the people, to "be shepherds with the smell of the sheep", as he put it at the Chrism Mass in 2013. In the exhortation he encourages all in the Church to go forth from "our own comfort zones in order to reach all the 'peripheries' in need of the light of the Gospel".[149]

In describing his intention for the document, Pope Francis says that he does not intend to give an exhaustive coverage of the topic or to address some of the more speculative issues, but rather to offer his thoughts on a number of issues that he sees as important. He lists them as follows:

---

146 *Evangelii Gaudium*, n. 3.
147 Ibid., n. 15.
148 He is quoting here from the *Aparecida Document*, nn. 548 and 370.
149 *Evangelii Gaudium*, n. 20.

- The reform of the Church in her missionary outreach.
- The temptations faced by pastoral workers.
- The Church, as the entire People of God, evanglises.
- The homily and its preparation.
- The inclusion of the poor in society.
- Peace and dialogue within society.
- The spiritual motivations for mission.

These, then, take up the bulk of his letter of exhortation.

Evangelii Gaudium is a document that gives a clear orientation to the purpose and mission of the Church. It continues in the tradition of teaching first presented in a fresh way by Pope Paul VI and built upon by Popes John Paul II and Benedict XVI. In the mind of the Church, expressed by a succession of popes in our time, the new evangelisation is to be the pastoral strategy for the Church in the third millennium.

Pope Francis from *Evangelii Gaudium* deserves the last word:

> Let us go forth, then, let us go forth to offer everyone the life of Jesus Christ. Here I repeat for the entire Church what I have often said to the priests and laity of Buenos Aires: I prefer a Church which is bruised, hurting and dirty because it has been out on the streets, rather than a Church which is unhealthy from being confined and from clinging to its own security.[150]

---

150 *Evangelii Gaudium*, n. 49.

www.ingramcontent.com/pod-product-compliance
Lightning Source LLC
Chambersburg PA
CBHW032250150426
43195CB00008BA/388